Allyn
and
Bacon

Research Navigator Guide

Speech Communication

Terrence Doyle

Northern Virginia Community College

Linda R. Barr

University of the Virgin Islands

PEARSON

Boston | New York | San Francisco
Mexico City | Montreal | Toronto | London | Madrid | Munich | Paris
Hong Kong | Singapore | Tokyo | Cape Town | Sydney

For related titles and support materials, visit our online catalog at
www.ablongman.com

Between the time Web site information is gathered and then published,
it is not unusual for some sites to have closed. Also, the transcription
of URLs can result in unintended typographical errors. The publisher
would appreciate notification where these errors occur so that they
may be corrected in subsequent editions.

ISBN   0-205-40864-8

Printed in the United States of America

10 9   08 07 06 05

Contents

Introduction

Your professor assigns a research paper or group report that's due in two weeks—and you need to make sure you have up-to-date, credible information. Where do you begin? Today, the easiest answer is the Internet—because it can be so convenient and there is so much information out there. But therein lies part of the problem. How do you know if the information is reliable and from a trustworthy source?

Research Navigator Guide: Speech Communication is designed to help you select and evaluate research from the Web to help you find the best and most credible information you can. Throughout this guide, you'll find:

- **A Quick Guide to Research Navigator.** All you need to know to get started with Research Navigator™, a research database that gives you immediate access to hundreds of scholarly journals and other popular publications, such as *Scientific American, U.S. News & World Report,* and many others.
- **A practical and to-the-point discussion of search engines.** Find out which search engines are likely to get you the information you want and how to phrase your searches for the most effective results.
- **Detailed information on evaluating online sources.** Locate credible information on the Web and get tips for thinking critically about Web sites.
- **Citation guidelines for Web resources.** Learn the proper citation guidelines for Web sites, email messages, listservs, and more.
- **Web activities for Speech Communication.** Explore the various ways you can use the Web in your courses through these online exercises.
- **Web links for Speech Communication.** Begin your Web research with the discipline-specific sources listed in this section. Also included is information about Web resources offered by Allyn & Bacon—these sites are designed to give you an extra boost in your speech communication courses.

So before running straight to your browser, take the time to read through this copy of *Research Navigator Guide: Speech Communication* and use it as a reference for all of your Web research needs.

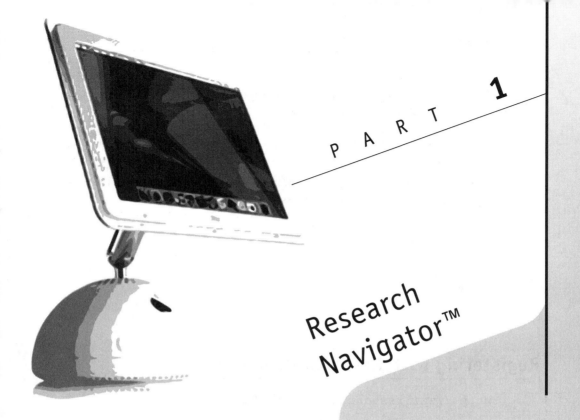

Research Navigator™

What Is Research Navigator™?

Research Navigator™ is the easiest way for you to start a research assignment or research paper. Complete with extensive help on the research process and three exclusive databases of credible and reliable source material (including EBSCO's ContentSelect™ Academic Journal and Abstract Database, *New York Times* Search by Subject Archive, and Link Library), Research Navigator™ helps you quickly and efficiently make the most of your research time.

Research Navigator™ includes three databases of dependable source material to get your research process started:

1. EBSCO's ContentSelect™ Academic Journal and Abstract Database, organized by subject, contains 50–100 of the leading academic journals per discipline. Instructors and students can search the online journals by keyword, topic, or multiple topics. Articles include abstract and citation information and can be cut, pasted, emailed, or saved for later use.
2. The *New York Times* Search by Subject Archive is organized by academic subject and searchable by keyword, or multiple keywords. Instructors and students can view full-text articles from the world's leading journalists from *The New York Times*. The *New York Times*

Search by Subject Archive is available exclusively to instructors and students through Research Navigator™.

3. Link Library, organized by subject, offers editorially selected "Best of the Web" sites. Link libraries are continually scanned and kept up to date, providing the most relevant and accurate links for research assignments.

In addition, Research Navigator™ includes extensive online content detailing the steps in the research process including:

- Starting the Research Process
- Finding and Evaluating Sources
- Citing Sources
- Internet Research
- Using your Library
- Starting to Write

Registering with Research Navigator™

`http://www.researchnavigator.com`

Research Navigator™ is simple to use and easy to navigate. The goal of Research Navigator™ is to help you complete research assignments or research papers quickly and efficiently. The site is organized around the following tabs:

- Home
- Research Process
- Finding Sources
- Using Your Library

In order to begin using Research Navigator™, you must first register using the personal access code that appears in the front cover of this book.

To Register:
4. Go to **http://www.researchnavigator.com**
5. Click "Register" under "New Users" on the left side of the screen.
6. Enter the access code exactly as it appears on the inside front cover of this book. (Note: Access codes can only be used once to complete one registration. If you purchased a used guide, the access code may not work. Please go to **www.researchnavigator.com** for information on how to obtain a new access code.)
7. Follow the instructions on screen to complete your registration—you may click the Help button at any time if you are unsure how to respond.
8. Once you have successfully completed registration, write down the Login Name and Password you just created and keep it in a safe place.

You will need to enter it each time you want to revisit Research Navigator™.

9. Once you register, you have access to all the resources in Research Navigator™ for twelve months.

Getting Started

From the Research Navigator™ homepage, you have easy access to all of the site's main features, including a quick route to the three exclusive databases of source content that will be discussed in greater detail on the following pages. If you are new to the research process, you may want to start by clicking the *Research Process* tab, located in the upper right hand section of the page. Here you will find extensive help on all aspects of the research process, including:

- Introduction to the Research Paper
- Gathering Data
- Searching the Internet
- Evaluating Sources
- Organizing Ideas
- Writing Notes
- Drafting the Paper
- Academic Citation Styles (MLA, APA, CME, and more)
- Blending Reference Material into Your Writing
- Practicing Academic Integrity
- Revising
- Proofreading
- Editing the Final Draft

For those of you who are already familiar with the research process, you already know that the first step in completing a research assignment or research paper is to select a topic. (In some cases, your instructor may assign you a topic.) According to James D. Lester in *Writing Research Papers,* choosing a topic for the research paper can be easy (any topic will serve) yet very complicated (an informed choice is critical). He suggests selecting a person, a person's work, or a specific issue to study—President George W. Bush, John Steinbeck's *Of Mice and Men,* or learned dexterity with Nintendo games. Try to select a topic that will meet three demands.

1. It must examine a significant issue.
2. It must address a knowledgeable reader and carry that reader to another level of knowledge.
3. It must have a serious purpose, one that demands analysis of the issues, argues from a position, and explains complex details.

You can find more tips from Lester in the *Research Process* section of Research Navigator™.

Research Navigator Guide: Speech Communication

Research Navigator™ simplifies your research efforts by giving you a convenient launching pad for gathering data on your topic. The site has aggregated three distinct types of source material commonly used in research assignments: academic journals (ContentSelect™); newspaper articles (*New York Times*) and world wide Web sites (Link Library).

EBSCO's ContentSelect Academic Journal and Abstract Database

EBSCO's ContentSelect Academic Journal and Abstract Database contains scholarly, peer-reviewed journals (like the *Journal of Clinical Psychology* or the *Journal of Anthropology*). A scholarly journal is an edited collection of articles written by various authors and is published several times per year. All the issues published in one calendar year comprise a volume of that journal. For example, the *American Sociological Review* published volume 65 in the year 2000. This official journal of the American Sociological Association is published six times a year, so issues 1–6 in volume 65 are the individual issues for that year. Each issue contains between 4 and 8 articles written by a variety of authors. Additionally, journal issues may contain letters from the editor, book reviews, and comments from authors. Each issue of a journal does not necessarily revolve around a common theme. In fact, most issues contain articles on many different topics.

Scholarly journals, are similar to magazines in that they are published several times per year and contain a variety of articles in each issue, however, they are NOT magazines. What sets them apart from popular magazines like *Newsweek* or *Science News* is that the content of each issue is peer-reviewed. This means that each journal has, in addition to an editor and editorial staff, a pool of reviewers. Rather than a staff of writers who write something on assignment, journals accept submissions from academic researchers all over the world. The editor relies on these peer reviewers both to evaluate the articles, which are submitted, and to decide if they should be accepted for publication. These published articles provide you with a specialized knowledge and information about your research topic. Academic journal articles adhere to strict scientific guidelines for methodology and theoretical grounding. The information obtained in these individual articles is more scientific than information you would find in a popular magazine, newspaper article, or on a Web page.

Using ContentSelect

Searching for articles in ContentSelect is easy! Here are some instructions and search tips to help you find articles for your research paper.

Step 1: **Select an academic subject and topic area.** When you first enter the ContentSelect Research Database, you will see a list of disciplines. To search within a single academic subject, click the name of that subject. In order to search in more than one academic subject, hold down the alt or command key. In the space below where all the subjects are listed, you must enter a topic area. For example if you choose Psychology as an academic subject you might enter "Freud" as a topic area.

Step 2: Click the **GO** button to start your search.

Step 3: **Basic Search.** By clicking **GO** you will be brought to the *Basic Search* tab. Basic Search lets you search for articles using a variety of methods. You can select from: Standard Search, All Words, Any Words, or Exact Phrase. For more information on these options, click the **<u>Search Tips</u>** link at any time!

Step 4: After you have selected your method Click **Search.**

Some ways to improve your search:

Tip 1: **Using AND, OR, and NOT** to help you search. In Standard Search, you can use AND, OR and NOT to create a very broad or very narrow search:

- **AND** searches for articles containing all of the words. For example, typing **education AND technology** will search for articles that contain **both** education AND technology.
- **OR** searches for articles that contains at least one of the terms. For example, searching for **education OR technology** will find articles that contain either education OR technology.
- **NOT** excludes words so that the articles will not include the word that follows "NOT." For example, searching for **education NOT technology** will find articles that contain the term education but NOT the term technology.

Tip 2: **Using All Words.** When you select the "All Words" option, you do not need to use the word AND—you will automatically search for articles that only contain all of the words. The order of the search words entered in does not matter. For example, typing **education technology** will search for articles that contain **both** education AND technology.

Tip 3: **Using Any Words.** After selecting the "Any Words" option, type words, a phrase, or a sentence in the window. ContentSelect will search for articles that contain any of the terms you typed (but will not search for words such as **in** and **the**). For example, type **rising medical costs in the United States** to find articles that contain *rising, medical, costs, United,* or *States.* To limit your search to find articles that contain exact terms, use *quotation marks*—for example, typing "United States" will only search for articles containing "United States."

Tip 4: **Using Exact Phrase.** Select this option to find articles containing an exact phrase. ContentSelect will search for articles that include all the words you entered, exactly as you entered them. For example, type **rising medical costs in the United States** to find articles that contain the exact phrase "rising medical costs in the United States."

Search by Article Number

Each and every article in EBSCO's ContentSelect Academic Journal and Abstract Database is assigned its own unique article number. In some instances, you may know the exact article number for the journal article you want to retrieve. Perhaps you noted it during a prior research session on Research Navigator™. Such article numbers might also be found on the companion web site for your text, or in the text itself.

To retrieve a specific article, simply type that article number in the "Search by Article Number" field and click the **GO** button.

Advanced Search

The following tips will help you with an Advanced Search.

Step 1: To switch to an **Advanced Search**, from the Basic Search click the *AdvancedSearch* tab on the navigation bar, just under the EBSCO Host logo. The *AdvancedSearch* tab helps you focus your search using keyword searching, search history and limiters.

Step 2: Type the words you want to search for in the **Find** field.

Step 3: Click on **Field Codes** to see a list of available field codes for limiting your search. For example: AU-Author, will limit your search to an author. Enter one of these two-letter field codes before your search term. For example, if you enter AU-Smith, this will limit your results to SMITH in the Author field. For more information on field codes, click **Search Tips**.

Step 4: After you have added the appropriate Field Code to your topic, click **Search.**

Some ways to improve your search:

Tip 1: You can enter additional search terms in the **Find** field, and remember to use *and, or,* and *not* to connect multiple search terms (see Tip 1 under Basic Search for information on *and, or,* and *not*).

Tip 2: With Advanced Searches you can also use **Limiters** and **Expanders** to refine your search. For more information on Limiters and Expanders, click **Search Tips**.

The *New York Times* Search by Subject Archive

Newspapers, also known as periodicals because they are issued in periodic installments (e.g. daily, weekly, or monthly), provide contemporary information. Information in periodicals—journals, magazines, and newspapers—may be useful, or even critical, when you are ready to focus in on specific aspects of your topic, or to find more up-to-date information.

There are some significant differences between newspaper articles and journal articles, and you should consider the level of scholarship that is most appropriate for your research. Popular or controversial topics may not be well covered in journals, even though coverage in newspapers and "general interest" magazines like *Newsweek* and *Science* for that same topic may be extensive.

Research Navigator™ gives you access to a one-year, "search by subject" archive of articles from one of the world's leading newspapers—*The New York Times.* To learn more about *The New York Times,* visit them on the Web at **http://www.nytimes.com**.

Using the search-by-subject archive is easy. Simply type a word, or multiple words separated by commas, into the search box and click "go." You will see a list of articles that have appeared in the *New York Times* over the last year, sorted by most recent article first. You can further refine your search as needed. Articles can be printed or saved for later use in your research assignment. Be sure to review the citation rules for how to cite a newspaper article in endnotes or a bibliography.

"Best of the Web" Link Library

The third database included on Research Navigator™, Link Library, is a collection of Web links, organized by academic subject and key terms. To use this database, simply select an academic subject from the dropdown list, and then find the key term for the topic you are searching. Click on the key term and see a list of five to seven editorially reviewed Web sites that offer educationally relevant and reliable content. For example, if your research topic is "Allergies," you may want to select the academic subject Biology and then click on "Allergies" for links to web sites that explore this topic. Simply click on the alphabet bar to view other key terms in Biology, and their corresponding links. The web links in Link Library are monitored and updated each week, reducing your incidence of finding "dead" links.

Using Your Library

After you have selected your topic and gathered source material from the three databases of content on Research Navigator™, you may need to complete your research by going to your school library. Research Navigator™ does not try to replace the library, but rather helps you understand how to use library resources effectively and efficiently.

You may put off going to the library to complete research assignments or research papers because the library can seem overwhelming. Research Navigator™ provides a bridge to the library by taking you through a simple step-by-step overview of how to make the most of your library time. Written by a library scientist, the *Using Your Library* tab explains:

• Major types of libraries
• What the library has to offer
• How to choose the right library tools for a project
• The research process
• How to make the most of research time in the library

In addition, when you are ready to use the library to complete a research assignment or research paper, Research Navigator™ includes 31 discipline-specific "library guides" for you to use as a roadmap. Each guide includes an overview of the discipline's major subject databases, online journals, and key associations and newsgroups.

For more information and detailed walk-throughs, please visit
www.ablongman.com/aboutRN

Research Navigator Guide: Speech Communication

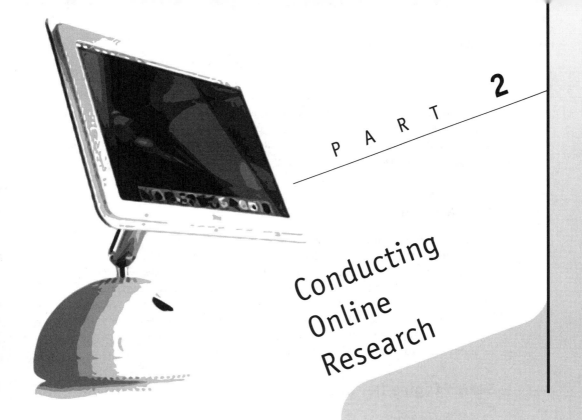

PART **2**

Conducting Online Research

Finding Sources:
Search Engines and Subject Directories

Your professor has just given you an assignment to give a five minute speech on the topic "gun control." After a (hopefully brief) panic attack, you begin to think of what type of information you need before you can write the speech. To provide an interesting introduction, you decide to involve your class by taking a straw poll of their views for and against gun control, and to follow this up by giving some statistics on how many Americans favor (and oppose) gun control legislation and then by outlining the arguments on both sides of the issue. If you already know the correct URL for an authoritative Web site like Gallup Opinion Polls (www.gallup.com) or other sites you are in great shape! However, what do you do when you don't have a clue as to which Web site would have information on your topic? In these cases, many, many people routinely (and mistakenly) go to Yahoo! and type in a single term (e.g., guns). This approach is sure to bring first a smile to your face when the results offer you 200,874 hits on your topic, but just as quickly make you grind your teeth in frustration when you start scrolling down the hit list and find sites that range from gun dealerships, to reviews of the video "Young Guns," to aging fan sites for "Guns and Roses."

Finding information on a specific topic on the Web is a challenge. The more intricate your research need, the more difficult it is to find the one or two Web sites among the billions that feature the information you want. This section is designed to help you to avoid frustration and to focus in on the right site for your research by using search engines, subject directories, and meta-sites.

Search Engines

Search engines (sometimes called search services) are becoming more numerous on the Web. Originally, they were designed to help users search the Web by topic. More recently, search engines have added features which enhance their usefulness, such as searching a particular part of the Web (e.g., only sites of educational institutions—dot.edu), retrieving just one site which the search engine touts as most relevant (like Ask Jeeves {www.aj.com}), or retrieving up to 10 sites which the search engine rank as most relevant (like Google {www.google.com}).

Search Engine Defined

According to Cohen (1999):

> "A search engine service provides a searchable database of Internet files collected by a computer program called a wanderer, crawler, robot, worm, or spider. Indexing is created from the collected files, and the results are presented in a schematic order. There are no selection criteria for the collection of files.
>
> A search service therefore consists of three components: (1) a spider, a program that traverses the Web from link to link, identifying and reading pages; (2) an index, a database containing a copy of each Web page gathered by the spider; and (3) a search engine mechanism, software that enables users to query the index and then returns results in a schematic order (p. 31)."

One problem students often have in their use of search engines is that they are deceptively easy to use. Like our example "guns," no matter what is typed into the handy box at the top, links to numerous Web sites appear instantaneously, lulling students into a false sense of security. Since so much was retrieved, surely SOME of it must be useful. WRONG! Many Web sites retrieved will be very light on substantive content, which is not what you need for most academic endeavors. Finding just the right Web site has been likened to finding diamonds in the desert.

As you can see by the definition above, one reason for this is that most search engines use indexes developed by machines. Therefore they are indexing terms not concepts. The search engine cannot tell the difference between the keyword "crack" to mean a split in the sidewalk and "crack" referring to crack cocaine. To use search engines properly takes some skill, and this chapter will provide tips to help you use search engines more effectively. First, however, let's look at the different types of search engines with examples:

TYPES OF SEARCH ENGINES		
TYPE	DESCRIPTION	EXAMPLES
1st Generation	• Non-evaluative, do not evaluate results in terms of content or authority. • Return results ranked by relevancy alone (number of times the term(s) entered appear, usually on the first paragraph or page of the site)	AltaVista (www.altavista.com/) Excite (www.excite.com) HotBot (www.HotBot.com) Infoseek (guide.infoseek.com) Ixquick Metasearch (ixquick.com) Lycos (www.lycos.com)
2nd Generation	• More creative in displaying results. • Results are ordered by characteristics such as: concept, document type, Web site, popularity, etc. rather than relevancy.	Ask Jeeves (www.aj.com/) Direct Hit (www.directhit.com/) Google! (www.google.com/) HotLinks (www.hotlinks.com/) Simplifind (www.simpli.com/) SurfWax (www.surfwax.com/) Also see Meta-Search engines below. EVALUATIVE SEARCH ENGINES About.Com (www.about.com) WebCrawler (www.webcrawler.com)
Commercial Portals	• Provide additional features such as: customized news, stock quotations, weather reports, shopping, etc. • They want to be used as a "one stop" Web guide. • They profit from prominent advertisements and fees charged to featured sites.	GONetwork (www.go.com/) Google Web Directory (directory.google.com/) LookSmart (www.looksmart.com/) My Starting Point (www.stpt.com/) Open Directory Project (dmoz.org/) NetNow (www.inetnow.com) Yahoo! (www.yahoo.com/)
Meta-Search Engines	Run searches on multiple search engines.	There are different types of meta-search engines. See the next 2 boxes.

(continued)

TYPES OF SEARCH ENGINES, *continued*		
TYPE	DESCRIPTION	EXAMPLES
Meta-Search Engines *Integrated Result*	• Display results for search engines in one list. • Duplicates are removed. • Only portions of results from each engine are returned.	Beaucoup.com (www.beaucoup.com/) Highway 61 (www.highway61.com) Cyber411(www.cyber411. com/) Mamma (www.mamma.com/) MetaCrawler (www. metacrawler.com/) Visisimo (www.vivisimo.com) Northern Light (www.nlsearch.com/) SurfWax (www.surfwax.com)
Meta-Search Engines *Non-Integrated Results*	• Comprehensive search. • Displays results from each search engine in separate results sets. • Duplicates remain. • You must sift through all the sites.	Dogpile (www.dogpile.com) Global Federated Search (jin.dis.vt.edu/fedsearch/) GoHip (www.gohip.com) Searchalot (www.searchalot.com) 1Blink (www.1blink.com) ProFusion (www. profusion.com/)

QUICK TIPS FOR MORE EFFECTIVE USE OF SEARCH ENGINES

1. Use a search engine:
   - When you have a narrow idea to search.
   - When you want to search the full text of countless Web pages
   - When you want to retrieve a large number of sites
   - When the features of the search engine (like searching particular parts of the Web) help with your search

2. Always use Boolean Operators to combine terms. Searching on a single term is a sure way to retrieve a very large number of Web pages, few, if any, of which are on target.
   - Always check search engine's HELP feature to see what symbols are used for the operators as these vary (e.g., some engines use the & or + symbol for AND).
   - Boolean Operators include:
   AND to narrow search and to make sure that **both** terms are included
       e.g:, children AND violence
   OR to broaden search and to make sure that **either** term is included
       e.g., child OR children OR juveniles
   NOT to **exclude** one term
       e.g., eclipse NOT lunar

3. Use appropriate symbols to indicate important terms and to indicate phrases (Best Bet for Constructing a Search According to Cohen (1999): Use a plus sign (+) in front of terms you want to retrieve: +solar +eclipse. Place a phrase in double quotation marks: "solar eclipse" Put together: "+solar eclipse" "+South America").

4. Use word stemming (a.k.a. truncation) to find all variations of a word (check search engine HELP for symbols).
   - If you want to retrieve child, child's, or children use child* (some engines use other symbols such as !, #, or $)
   - Some engines automatically search singular and plural terms, check HELP to see if yours does.

5. Since search engines only search a portion of the Web, use several search engines or a meta-search engine to extend your reach.

6. Remember search engines are generally mindless drones that do not evaluate. Do not rely on them to find the best Web sites on your topic, use *subject directories* or meta-sites to enhance value (see below).

Finding Those Diamonds in the Desert: Using Subject Directories and Meta-sites

Although some search engines, like WebCrawler (www.webcrawler.com) do evaluate the Web sites they index, most search engines do not make any judgment on the worth of the content. They just return a long—sometimes very long—list of sites that contained your keyword. However, *subject directories* exist that are developed by human indexers, usually librarians or subject experts, and are defined by Cohen (1999) as follows:

> "A subject directory is a service that offers a collection of links to Internet resources submitted by site creators or evaluators and organized into subject categories. Directory services use selection criteria for choosing links to include, though the selectivity varies among services (p. 27)."

World Wide Web Subject directories are useful when you want to see sites on your topic that have been reviewed, evaluated, and selected for their authority, accuracy, and value. They can be real time savers for students, since subject directories weed out the commercial, lightweight, or biased Web sites.

Metasites are similar to subject directories, but are more specific in nature, usually dealing with one scholarly field or discipline. Some examples of subject directories and meta-sites are found in the table on the next page.

Choose subject directories to ensure that you are searching the highest quality Web pages. As an added bonus, subject directories periodically check Web links to make sure that there are fewer dead ends and out-dated links.

SMART SEARCHING—SUBJECT DIRECTORIES AND META-SITES

TYPES—SUBJECT DIRECTORIES	EXAMPLES
General, covers many topics	Access to Internet and Subject Resources (www2.lib.udel.edu/subj/) Best Information on the Net (BIOTN) (http://library.sau.edu/bestinfo/) Federal Web Locator (www.infoctr.edu/fwl/) Galaxy (galaxy.einet.net) INFOMINE: Scholarly Internet Resource Collections (infomine.ucr.edu/) InfoSurf: Resources by Subject (www.library.ucsb.edu/subj/) Librarian's Index to the Internet (www.lii.org/) Martindale's "The Reference Desk" (www-sci.lib.uci.edu/HSG/ref.html) PINAKES: A Subject Launchpad (www.hw.ac.uk/libWWW/irn/pinakes/pinakes.html) Refdesk.com (www.refdesk.com) Search Engines and Subject Directories (College of New Jersey) (www.tcnj.edu/~library/research/internet_search.html) Scout Report Archives (www.scout.cs.wisc.edu/archives) Selected Reference Sites (www.mnsfld.edu/depts/lib/mu~ref.html) WWW Virtual Library (http://vlib.org)
Subject Oriented	
• Communication Studies	The Media and Communication Studies Site (www.aber.ac.uk/media) University of Iowa Department of Communication Studies (www.uiowa.edu/~commstud/resources)
• Cultural Studies	Sara Zupko's Cultural Studies Center (www.popcultures.com)
• Education	Educational Virtual Library (www.csu.edu.au/education/library.html) ERIC [Education ResourcesInformation Center] (ericir.sunsite.syr.edu/) Kathy Schrock's Guide for Educators (kathyschrock.net/abceval/index.htm)
• Journalism	Journalism Resources (bailiwick.lib.uiowa.edu/journalism/) Journalism and Media Criticism page (www.chss.montclair.edu/english/furr/media.html)
• Literature	Norton Web Source to American Literature (www.wwnorton.com/naal) Project Gutenberg [Over 3,000 full text titles] (www.gutenberg.net)

SMART SEARCHING, *continued*	
TYPES—SUBJECT DIRECTORIES	EXAMPLES
• Medicine & Health	PubMed [National Library of Medicine's index to Medical journals, 1966 to present] (www.ncbi.nlm.nih.gov/PubMed/)
	RxList: The Internet Drug Index (rxlist.com)
	Go Ask Alice (www.goaskalice.columbia.edu) [Health and sexuality]
• Technology	CNET.com (www.cnet.com)

Another closely related group of sites are the *Virtual Library sites,* also referred to as Digital Library sites. Hopefully, your campus library has an outstanding Web site for both on-campus and off-campus access to resources. If not, there are several virtual library sites that you can use, although you should realize that some of the resources would be subscription based, and not accessible unless you are a student of that particular university or college. These are useful because, like the subject directories and meta-sites, experts have organized Web sites by topic and selected only those of highest quality.

You now know how to search for information and use search engines more effectively. In the next section, you will learn more tips for evaluating the information that you found.

VIRTUAL LIBRARY SITES	
PUBLIC LIBRARIES	
• Internet Public Library	www.ipl.org
• Library of Congress	lcweb.loc.gov/homepage/lchp.html
• New York Public Library	www.nypl.org
University/College Libraries	
• Bucknell	jade.bucknell.edu/
• Case Western	www.cwru.edu/uclibraries.html
• Dartmouth	www.dartmouth.edu/~library
• Duke	www.lib.duke.edu/
• Franklin & Marshall	www.library.fandm.edu
• Harvard	www.harvard.edu/museums/
• Penn State	www.libraries.psu.edu
• Princeton	infoshare1.princeton.edu
• Stanford	www.slac.stanford.edu/FIND/spires.html
• ULCA	www.library.ucla.edu

(continued)

PUBLIC LIBRARIES

Other
*   Perseus Project [subject specific—classics, supported by   www.perseus.tufts.edu
    grants from corporations and educational institutions]

BIBLIOGRAPHY FOR FURTHER READING

Books

Basch, Reva. (1996). Secrets of the Super Net Searchers.

Berkman, Robert I. (2000). *Find It Fast: How to Uncover Expert Information on Any Subject Online or in Print*. NY: HarperResource.

Glossbrenner, Alfred & Glossbrenner, Emily. (1999). *Search Engines for the World Wide Web,* 2nd Ed. Berkeley, CA: Peachpit Press.

Hock, Randolph, & Berinstein, Paula.. (1999). *The Extreme Searcher's Guide to Web Search Engines: A Handbook for the Serious Searcher*. Information Today, Inc.

Miller, Michael. *Complete Idiot's Guide to Yahoo!* (2000). Indianapolis, IN: Que.

Miller, Michael. *Complete Idiot's Guide to Online Search Secrets*. (2000). Indianapolis, IN: Que.

Paul, Nora, Williams, Margot, & Hane, Paula. (1999). *Great Scouts!: CyberGuides for Subject Searching on the Web*. Information Today, Inc.

Radford, Marie, Barnes, Susan, & Barr, Linda (2001). *Web Research: Selecting, Evaluating, and Citing* Boston. Allyn and Bacon.

Journal Articles

Cohen, Laura B. (1999, August). The Web as a research tool: Teaching strategies for instructors. *CHOICE Supplement* 3, 20–44.

Cohen, Laura B. (August 2000). Searching the Web: The Human Element Emerges. *CHOICE Supplement 37,* 17–31.

Introna, Lucas D., & Nissenbaum, Helen. (2000). Shaping the web: Why the politics of search engines matters. The Information Society, Vol. 16, No. 3, pp. 169–185.

Evaluating Sources on the Web

Congratulations! You've found a great Web site. Now what? The Web site you found seems like the perfect Web site for your research. But, are you sure? Why is it perfect? What criteria are you using to determine whether this Web site suits your purpose?

Think about it. Where else on earth can anyone "publish" information regardless of the *accuracy, currency,* or *reliability* of the information? The

Research Navigator Guide: Speech Communication

Internet has opened up a world of opportunity for posting and distributing information and ideas to virtually everyone, even those who might post misinformation for fun, or those with ulterior motives for promoting their point of view. Armed with the information provided in this guide, you can dig through the vast amount of useless information and misinformation on the World Wide Web to uncover the valuable information. Because practically anyone can post and distribute their ideas on the Web, you need to develop a new set of *critical thinking skills* that focus on the evaluation of the quality of information, rather than be influenced and manipulated by slick graphics and flashy moving java script.

Before the existence of online sources, the validity and accuracy of a source was more easily determined. For example, in order for a book to get to the publishing stage, it must go through many critiques, validation of facts, reviews, editorial changes and the like. Ownership of the information in the book is clear because the author's name is attached to it. The publisher's reputation is on the line too. If the book turns out to have incorrect information, reputations and money can be lost. In addition, books available in a university library are further reviewed by professional librarians and selected for library purchase because of their accuracy and value to students. Journal articles downloaded or printed from online subscription services, such as Infotrac, ProQuest, EbscoHost, or other fulltext databases, are put through the same scrutiny as the paper versions of the journals.

On the World Wide Web, however, Internet service providers (ISPs) simply give Web site authors a place to store information. The Web site author can post information that may not be validated or tested for accuracy. One mistake students typically make is to assume that all information on the Web is of equal value. Also, in the rush to get assignments in on time, students may not take the extra time to make sure that the information they are citing is accurate. It is easy just to cut and paste without really thinking about the content in a critical way. However, to make sure you are gathering accurate information and to get the best grade on your assignments, it is vital that you develop your critical ability to sift through the dirt to find the diamonds.

Web Evaluation Criteria

So, here you are, at this potentially great site. Let's go though some ways you can determine if this site is one you can cite with confidence in your research. Keep in mind, ease of use of a Web site is an issue, but more important is learning how to determine the validity of data, facts, and statements for your use. The five traditional ways to verify a paper source can also be applied to your Web source: *accuracy, authority, objectivity, coverage,* and *currency.*

Evaluating Web Sites Using
Five Criteria to Judge Web Site Content

Accuracy—How reliable is the information?

Authority—Who is the author and what are his or her credentials?

Objectivity—Does the Web site present a balanced or biased point of view?

Coverage—Is the information comprehensive enough for your needs?

Currency—Is the Web site up to date?

Use additional criteria to judge Web site content, including

- **Publisher, documentation, relevance, scope, audience, appropriateness of format,** and **navigation**
- Judging whether the site is made up of **primary (original) or secondary (interpretive) sources**
- Determining whether the information is **relevant** to your research

Content Evaluation

Accuracy. Internet searches are not the same as searches of library databases because much of the information on the Web has not been edited, whereas information in databases has. It is your responsibility to make sure that the information you use in a school project is accurate. When you examine the content on a Web site or Web page, you can ask yourself a number of questions to determine whether the information is accurate.

1. Is the information reliable?
2. Do the facts from your other research contradict the facts you find on this Web page?
3. Do any misspellings and/or grammar mistakes indicate a hastily put together Web site that has not been checked for accuracy?
4. Is the content on the page verifiable through some other source? Can you find similar facts elsewhere (journals, books, or other online sources) to support the facts you see on this Web page?
5. Do you find links to other Web sites on a similar topic? If so, check those links to ascertain whether they back up the information you see on the Web page you are interested in using.
6. Is a bibliography of additional sources for research provided? Lack of a bibliography doesn't mean the page isn't accurate, but having one allows you further investigation points to check the information.
7. Does the site of a research document or study explain how the data was collected and the type of research method used to interpret the data?

If you've found a site with information that seems too good to be true, it may be. You need to verify information that you read on the Web by cross-checking against other sources.

Authority.   An important question to ask when you are evaluating a Web site is, "Who is the author of the information?" Do you know whether the author is a recognized authority in his or her field? Biographical information, references to publications, degrees, qualifications, and organizational affiliations can help to indicate an author's authority. For example, if you are researching the topic of laser surgery citing a medical doctor would be better than citing a college student who has had laser surgery.

The organization sponsoring the site can also provide clues about whether the information is fact or opinion. Examine how the information was gathered and the research method used to prepare the study or report. Other questions to ask include:

1. Who is responsible for the content of the page? Although a webmaster's name is often listed, this person is not necessarily responsible for the content.
2. Is the author recognized in the subject area? Does this person cite any other publications he or she has authored?
3. Does the author list his or her background or credentials (e.g., Ph.D. degree, title such as professor, or other honorary or social distinction)?
4. Is there a way to contact the author? Does the author provide a phone number or email address?
5. If the page is mounted by an organization, is it a known, reputable one?
6. How long has the organization been in existence?
7. Does the URL for the Web page end in the extension .edu or .org? Such extensions indicate authority compared to dotcoms (.com), which are commercial enterprises. (For example, www.cancer.com takes you to an online drugstore that has a cancer information page; www.cancer.org is the American Cancer Society Web site.)

A good idea is to ask yourself whether the author or organization presenting the information on the Web is an authority on the subject. If the answer is no, this may not be a good source of information.

Objectivity.   Every author has a point of view, and some views are more controversial than others. Journalists try to be objective by providing both sides of a story. Academics attempt to persuade readers by presenting a logical argument, which cites other scholars' work. You need to look for two sided arguments in news and information sites. For academic papers, you need to determine how the paper fits within its discipline and whether the author is using controversial methods for reporting a conclusion.

Authoritative authors situate their work within a larger discipline. This background helps readers evaluate the author's knowledge on a particular

Research Navigator Guide: Speech Communication

subject. You should ascertain whether the author's approach is controversial and whether he or she acknowledges this. More important, is the information being presented as fact or opinion? Authors who argue for their position provide readers with other sources that support their arguments. If no sources are cited, the material may be an opinion piece rather than an objective presentation of information. The following questions can help you determine objectivity:

1. Is the purpose of the site clearly stated, either by the author or the organization authoring the site?
2. Does the site give a balanced viewpoint or present only one side?
3. Is the information directed toward a specific group of viewers?
4. Does the site contain advertising?
5. Does the copyright belong to a person or an organization?
6. Do you see anything to indicate who is funding the site?

Everyone has a point of view. This is important to remember when you are using Web resources. A question to keep asking yourself is, What is the bias or point of *view* being expressed here?

Coverage.   Coverage deals with the breadth and depth of information presented on a Web site. Stated another way, it is about how much information is presented and how detailed the information is. Looking at the site map or index can give you an idea about how much information is contained on a site. This isn't necessarily bad. Coverage is a criteria that is tied closely to *your* research requirement. For one assignment, a given Web site may be too general for your needs. For another assignment, that same site might be perfect. Some sites contain very little actual information because pages are filled with links to other sites. Coverage also relates to objectivity You should ask the following questions about coverage:

1. Does the author present both sides of the story or is a piece of the story missing?
2. Is the information comprehensive enough for your needs?
3. Does the site cover too much, too generally?
4. Do you need more specific information than the site can provide?
5. Does the site have an objective approach?

In addition to examining what is covered on a Web site, equally revealing is what is not covered. Missing information can reveal a bias in the material. Keep in mind that you are evaluating the information on a Web site for your research requirements.

Currency.   Currency questions deal with the timeliness of information. However, currency is more important for some topics than for others. For example, currency is essential when you are looking for technology related topics and current events. In contrast, currency may not be relevant when you are doing research on Plato or Ancient Greece. In terms of Web sites, currency also pertains to whether the site is being kept up to date and links are being maintained. Sites on the Web are sometimes abandoned by their owners. When people move or change jobs, they may neglect to remove theft site from the company or university server. To test currency ask the following questions:

1. Does the site indicate when the content was created?
2. Does the site contain a last revised date? How old is the date? (In the early part of 2001, a university updated their Web site with a "last up-dated" date of 1901! This obviously was a Y2K problem, but it does point out the need to be observant of such things!)
3. Does the author state how often he or she revises the information? Some sites are on a monthly update cycle (e.g., a government statistics page).
4. Can you tell specifically what content was revised?
5. Is the information still useful for your topic? Even if the last update is old, the site might still be worthy of use *if* the content is still valid for your research.

Relevancy to Your Research: Primary versus Secondary Sources

Some research assignments require the use of primary (original) sources. Materials such as raw data, diaries, letters, manuscripts, and original accounts of events can be considered primary material. In most cases, these historical documents are no longer copyrighted. The Web is a great source for this type of resource.

Information that has been analyzed and previously interpreted is considered a secondary source. Sometimes secondary sources are more appropriate than primary sources. If, for example, you are asked to analyze a topic or to find an analysis of a topic, a secondary source of an analysis would be most appropriate. Ask yourself the following questions to determine whether the Web site is relevant to your research:

1. Is it a primary or secondary source?
2. Do you need a primary source?
3. Does the assignment require you to cite different types of sources? For example, are you supposed to use at least one book, one journal article, and one Web page?

You need to think critically, both visually and verbally, when evaluating Web sites. Because Web sites are designed as multimedia hypertexts, nonlinear texts, visual elements, and navigational tools are added to the evaluation process.

Help in Evaluating Web Sites.   One shortcut to finding high-quality Web sites is using subject directories and meta-sites, which select the Web sites they index by similar evaluation criteria to those just described. If you want to learn more about evaluating Web sites, many colleges and universities provide sites that help you evaluate Web resources. The following list contains some excellent examples of these evaluation sites:

- Evaluating Quality on the Net—Hope Tillman, Babson College
  www.hopetillman.com/findqual.html
- Critical Web Evaluation—Kurt W. Wagner, William Paterson University of New Jersey
  euphrates.wpunj.edu/faculty/wagnerk/
- Evalation Criteria—Susan Beck, New Mexico State University
  lib.nmsu.edu/instruction/evalcrit.html
- A Student's Guide to Research with the WWW
  www.slu.edu/departments/english/research/
- Evaluating Web Pages: Questions to Ask & Strategies for Getting the Answers
  www.lib.berkeley.edu/TeachingLib/Guides/Internet/EvalQuestions.html

Critical Evaluation Web Sites

WEB SITE AND URL	SOURCE
Critical Thinking in an Online World **www.library.ucsb.edu/untangle/jones.html**	*Paper from "Untangling the Web" 1996*
Educom Review: Information **www.educause.edu/pub/er/review/reviewArticles/31231.html**	*EDUCAUSE Literacy as a Liberal Art (1996 article)*
Evaluating Information Found on the Internet **MiltonsWeb.mse.jhu.edu/research/education/net.html**	*University of Utah Library*
Evaluating Web Sites **www.lib.purdue.edu/InternetEval**	*Purdue University Library*
Evaluating Web Sites **www.lehigh.edu/~inref/guides/evaluating.web.html**	*Lehigh University*
ICONnect: Curriculum Connections Overview **www.ala.org/ICONN/evaluate.html**	*American Library Association's technology education initiative*
Kathy Schrock's ABC's of Web Site Evaluation **www.kathyschrock.net/abceval/**	*Author's Web site*

Kids Pick the best of the Web "Top 10: Announced" **www.ala.org/news/topkidpicks.html**	*American Library Association initiative underwritten by Microsoft (1998)*
Resource Selection and Information Evaluation **alexia.lis.uiuc.edu/~janicke/ InfoAge.html**	*Univ of Illinois, Champaign- Urbana (Librarian)*
Testing the Surf: Criteria for Evaluating Internet Information Sources **info.lib.uh.edu/pr/v8/n3/ smit8n3.html**	*University of Houston Libraries*
Evaluating Web Resources **www2.widener.edu/ Wolfgram-Memorial-Library/ webevaluation/webeval.htm**	*Widener University Library*
UCLA College Library Instruction: Thinking Critically about World Wide Web Resources **www.library.ucla.edu/libraries/ college/help/critical/**	*UCLA Library*
UG OOL: Judging Quality on the Internet **www.open.uoguelph.ca/resources/ skills/judging.html**	*University of Guelph*
Web Evaluation Criteria **lib.nmsu.edu/instruction/ evalcrit.html**	*New Mexico State University Library*
Web Page Credibility Checklist **www.park.pvt.k12.md.us/academics/ research/credcheck.htm**	*Park School of Baltimore*
Evaluating Web Sites for Educational Uses: Bibliography and Checklist **www.unc.edu/cit/guides/irg-49.html**	*University of North Carolina*
Evaluating Web Sites **www.lesley.edu/library/guides/ research/evaluating_web.html**	*Lesley University*

> *Tip:* Can't seem to get a URL to work? If the URL doesn't begin with www, you may need to put the http:// in front of the URL. Usually, browsers can handle URLs that begin with www without the need to type in the "http://" but if you find you're having trouble, add the http://.

Research Navigator Guide: Speech Communication

Documentation Guidelines for Online Sources

Your Citation for Exemplary Research

There's another detail left for us to handle—the formal citing of electronic sources in academic papers. The very factor that makes research on the Internet exciting is the same factor that makes referencing these sources challenging: their dynamic nature. A journal article exists, either in print or on microfilm, virtually forever. A document on the Internet can come, go, and change without warning. Because the purpose of citing sources is to allow another scholar to retrace your argument, a good citation allows a reader to obtain information from your primary sources, to the extent possible. This means you need to include not only information on when a source was posted on the Internet (if available) but also when you obtained the information.

The two arbiters of form for academic and scholarly writing are the Modern Language Association (MLA) and the American Psychological Association (APA); both organizations have established styles for citing electronic publications.

MLA Style

In the fifth edition of the *MLA Handbook for Writers of Research Papers,* the MLA recommends the following formats:

- **URLs:** URLs are enclosed in angle brackets (<>) and contain the access mode identifier, the formal name for such indicators as "http" or "ftp." If a URL must be split across two lines, break it only after a slash (/). Never introduce a hyphen at the end of the first line. The URL should include all the parts necessary to identify uniquely the file/document being cited.

  <http://www.csun.edu/~rtvfdept/home/index.html>

- **An online scholarly project or reference database:** A complete "online reference contains the title of the project or database (underlined); the name of the editor of the project or database (if given); electronic publication information, including version number (if relevant and if not part of the title), date of electronic publication or latest update, and name of any sponsoring institution or organization; date of access; and electronic address.

  <u>The Perseus Project</u>. Ed. Gregory R. Crane. Mar. 1997. Department of Classics, Tufts University. 15 June 1998 <http://www.perseus.tufts.edu/>.

If you cannot find some of the information, then include the information that is available. The MLA also recommends that you print or download electronic documents, freezing them in time for future reference.

- **A document within a scholarly project or reference database:** It is much more common to use only a portion of a scholarly project or database. To cite an essay, poem, or other short work, begin this citation with the name of the author and the title of the work (in quotation marks). Then, include all the information used when citing a complete online scholarly project or reference database, however, make sure you use the URL of the specific work and not the address of the general site.

Cuthberg, Lori. "Moonwalk: Earthlings' Finest Hour."
  <u>Discovery Channel Online</u>. 1999. Discovery
  Channel. 25 Nov. 1999 <http://www.discovery.com/
  indep/newsfeatures/moonwalk/challenge.html>.

- **A professional or personal site:** Include the name of the person creating the site (reversed), followed by a period, the title of the site (underlined), or, if there is no title, a description such as Home page (such a description is neither placed in quotes nor underlined). Then, specify the name of any school, organization, or other institution affiliated with the site and follow it with your date of access and the URL of the page.

Packer, Andy. Home page. 1Apr. 1998 <http://
  www.suu.edu/~students/Packer.htm>.

Some electronic references are truly unique to the online domain. These include email, newsgroup postings, MUDs (multiuser domains) or MOOs (multiuser domains, object-oriented), and IRCs (Internet Relay Chats).

Email. In citing email messages, begin with the writer's name (reversed) followed by a period, then the title of the message (if any) in quotations as it appears in the subject line. Next comes a description of the message, typically "Email to," and the recipient (e.g., "the author"), and finally the date of the message.

Davis, Jeffrey. "Web Writing Resources." Email to
  Nora Davis. 3 Jan. 2000.

Sommers, Laurice. "Re: College Admissions
  Practices." Email to the author. 12 Aug. 1998.

Research Navigator Guide: Speech Communication

List Servers and Newsgroups.   In citing these references, begin with the author's name (reversed) followed by a period. Next include the title of the document (in quotes) from the subject line, followed by the words "Online posting" (not in quotes). Follow this with the date of posting. For list servers, include the date of access, the name of the list (if known), and the online address of the list's moderator or administrator. For newsgroups, follow "Online posting" with the date of posting, the date of access, and the name of the newsgroup, prefixed with "news:" and enclosed in angle brackets.

```
Applebaum, Dale. "Educational Variables." Online
    posting. 29 Jan. 1998. Higher Education
    Discussion Group. 30 Jan. 1993
    <jlucidoj@unc.edu>.
```

```
Gostl, Jack. "Re: Mr. Levitan." Online posting.
    13 June 1997. 20 June 1997
    <news:alt.edu.bronxscience>.
```

MUDs, MOOs, and IRCs.   Begin with the name of the speaker(s) followed by a period. Follow with the description and date of the event, the forum in which the communication took place, the date of access, and the online address. If you accessed the MOO or MUD through telnet, your citation might appear as follows:

```
Guest. Personal interview. 13 Aug. 1998.
    <telnet://du.edu:8888>.
```

For more information on MLA documentation style for online sources, check out their Web site at http://www.mla.org/style/sources.htm.

APA Style

The newly revised *Publication Manual of the American Psychological Association* (5th ed.) now includes guidelines for Internet resources. The manual recommends that, at a minimum, a reference of an Internet source should provide a document title or description, a date (either the date of publication or update or the date of retrieval), and an address (in Internet terms, a uniform resource locator, or URL). Whenever possible, identify the authors of a document as well. It's important to remember that, unlike the MLA, the APA does not include temporary or transient sources (e.g., letters, phone calls, etc.) in its "References" page, preferring to handle them in the text. The general suggested format is as follows:

Online periodical:

Author, A. A., Author, B. B., & Author, C. C.
    (2000). Title of article. *Title of Periodical,*
    xx, xxxxx. Retrieved month, day, year, from
    source.

Online document:

Author, A. A. (2000). *Title of work.* Retrieved
    month, day, year, from source.

Some more specific examples are as follows:

FTP (File Transfer Protocol) Sites.   To cite files available for downloading via FTP, give the author's name (if known), the publication date (if available and if different from the date accessed), the full title of the paper (capitalizing only the first word and proper nouns), the date of access, and the address of the FTP site along with the full path necessary to access the file.

Deutsch, P. (1991) Archie: An electronic directory
    service for the Internet. Retrieved January 25,
    2000 from File Transfer Protocol: ftp://
    ftp.sura.net/pub/archie/docs/whatis.archie

WWW Sites (World Wide Web).   To cite files available for viewing or downloading via the World Wide Web, give the author's name (if known), the year of publication (if known and if different from the date accessed), the full title of the article, and the title of the complete work (if applicable) in italics. Include any additional information (such as versions, editions, or revisions) in parentheses immediately following the title. Include the date of retrieval and full URL (the http address).

Burka, L. P. (1993). A hypertext history of multi-
    user dungeons. *MUDdex.* Retrieved January 13, 1997
    from the World Wide Web: http://www.utopia.com/
    talent/lpb/muddex/essay/

Tilton, J. (1995). Composing good HTML (Vers. 2.0.6).
    Retrieved December 1, 1996 from the World Wide Web:
    http://www.cs.cmu.edu/~tilt/cgh/

Synchronous Communications (MOOs, MUDs, IRC, etc.).   Give the name of the speaker(s), the complete date of the conversation being referenced in parentheses, and the title of the session (if applicable). Next, list the title of the site in italics, the protocol and address (if applicable), and any directions necessary to access the work. Last, list the date of access, followed by the retrieval information. Personal interviews do not need to be listed in the References, but do need to be included in parenthetic references in the text (see the APA *Publication Manual*).

```
Cross, J. (1996, February 27). Netoric's Tuesday
    "cafe: Why use MUDs in the writing classroom?
    MediaMoo. Retrieved March 1, 1996 from File
    Transfer Protocol: ftp://daedalus.com/
    pub/ACW/NETORIC/catalog
```

Gopher Sites.   List the author's name (if applicable), the year of publication, the title of the file or paper, and the title of the complete work (if applicable). Include any print publication information (if available) followed by the protocol (i.e., gopher://). List the date that the file was accessed and the path necessary to access the file.

```
Massachusetts Higher Education Coordinating Council.
    (1994). Using coordination and collaboration to
    address change. Retrieved July 16, 1999 from the
    World Wide Web: gopher://gopher.mass.edu:170/
    00gopher_root%3A%5B_hecc%5D_plan
```

Email, Listservs, and Newsgroups.   Do not include personal email in the list of References. Although unretrievable communication such as email is not included in APA References, somewhat more public or accessible Internet postings from newsgroups or listservs may be included. See the APA *Publication Manual* for information on in-text citations.

```
Heilke, J. (1996, May 3). Webfolios. Alliance for
    Computers and Writing Discussion List. Retrieved
    December 31, 1996 from the World Wide Web:
    http://www.ttu.edu/lists/acw-1/9605/0040.html
```

Other authors and educators have proposed similar extensions to the APA style. You can find links to these pages at:

www.psychwww.com/resource/apacrib.htm

Remember, "frequently-referenced" does not equate to "correct" "or even "desirable." Check with your professor to see if your course or school has a preference for an extended APA style.

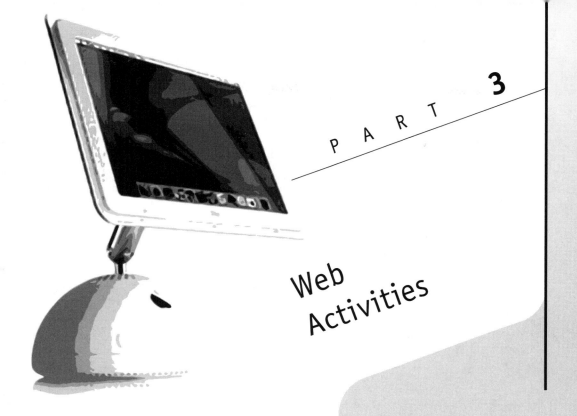

P A R T **3**

Web Activities

Internet Activities for Speech Communication

This section includes online activities that will explore some of the ways you can use the Internet in your course.

In this section, we will examine some of the ways that you can use the Internet to learn more about different aspects of speech communication. We will call this our Virtual Tour of Speech Communication. Our tour will encompass several activities:

1. Examine your day-to-day communications
2. Explore issues in interpersonal communication
3. Identify resources for studying workplace communication

Examine Your Day-to-Day Communications

How successfully do you communicate on a daily basis? That question was at the heart of a research study that was conducted by the Roper Organization. The study, entitled "How Americans Communicate," was sponsored by the National Communication Association. You can find a copy of the report by going to **http://www.natcom.org/research/Roper/how_americans_communicate.htm**.

Scroll down to the portion of the page that is given the subtitle, "Methods of Communicating that Americans Prefer." Observe how the study analyzed our comfort level in talking with others face-to-face, speaking on the phone, putting ideas into written form, participating at a meeting, giving a presentation or speech and interacting on the Internet. What is your comfort level in these types of daily communications? In the blanks below make a list of your communication preferences and then comment upon how and why each type of communication is comfortable or uncomfortable.

1. My most comfortable type of communication is:

_____

2. The second most comfortable type of communication is:

_____

3. The third most comfortable type of communication is:

_____

4. The fourth most comfortable type of communication is:

_____

5. The fifth most comfortable type of communication is:

_____

6. The sixth most comfortable type of communication is:

_____

Explore Issues in Interpersonal Communication

Locate Interpersonal Communication Research Materials

Interpersonal communication scholars and students focus on how we relate to one another in a variety of contexts. The formal study of interpersonal communication also draws from a wide range of related, interdisciplinary fields such as psychology, sociology, anthropology, philosophy, language studies and media criticism. To identify some of the types of resources you can find for studying interpersonal communication, we will use a Web site called the Interpersonal Web. Visit it at **http://novaonline.nv.cc.va.us/ eli/spd110td/interper/index.html/**.

The Interpersonal Web provides a collection of resources that are grouped into six headings: culture, types of relationships, self, relational development, verbal and nonverbal messages, and listening and perception. Explore the site by choosing one of its six major headings. Then, answer the following questions.

1. Which heading did you select? How is this subtopic of interpersonal communication studies related to your interests and experiences of relating to others?

_____

_____

_____

2. Next, click on the icon in the lower right hand corner of the page that identifies "Research Questions." Explore the list of research questions and some of the links that are provided as starters for doing research in that area of interpersonal communication. Which research topic did you select? What are some of the resources that you found that would be valuable for pursuing further investigations on that topic?

_____

_____

_____

Learn from Interactive Exercises

You can gain insight about how you communicate interpersonally by doing surveys that are available online. Most of these are based on research in interpersonal communication concepts. They may also be a great deal of fun! Pick one of the following surveys that has the most pertinence and interest to you.

- **Body Image:** Do you have a body image problem?
  http://quiz.ivillage.com/substance/tests/body.htm
- **Friendship:** What is your friendship style?
  http://quiz.ivillage.com/health/tests.friendstyle.htm
- **Romantic Relationships:** What kind of lover are you?
  http://quiz.ivillage.com/relationshipstests/luvtest.htm
- **Listening:** Listening Self-Assessment
  http://www.highgain.com/SELF/index.php3
- **Spatial Communication:** What is your decorating attitude?
  http://www.bhg.com/househome/quiz/

1. What did the interactive survey teach you about yourself and how you communicate?

_____

_____

_____

2. Did the information you found in the survey relate to some of the principles of communication that you are studying in your speech communication course? How?

_____

_____

_____

Locate Expert Guides

Expert guides perform a valuable editorial function on the Web by locating and screening resources. One of the most useful sources for finding expert guides on various topics related to interpersonal communication is About.com. Visit the About.com page for relationships at **http://home. about.com/people.**

1. Which topics on this portal site have the most pertinence to your study of interpersonal communication?

_____

_____

_____

Locate Resources for Workplace Communication: Interviewing and Small Group Interaction

Learn More about Interviewing

Skill at interviewing is very important for your career and success at communicating in the workplace. For this activity, check out a couple of useful links that can help you identify the types of skills that you will need to be able to interview well. Begin with the College Grad Job Hunter. Go to **http://www.collegegrad.com/index.shtml**.

1. What are the most important principles of communication that you need to master to be successful when you interview for a job?

_____

_____

_____

Next, examine a communication site that provides a tutorial for developing your communication skills. Visit the Virtual Interviewing Assistant, which was developed at the University of Kansas. Go to **http://www. ukans.edu/cwis/units/coms2/via/**.

Research Navigator Guide: Speech Communication

In particular, consider the communication influences on the interviewer and interviewee that affect outcome of interviews and how you develop your strategies for preparing and participating in interviews.

1. What are some of the most important influences?

_____

_____

_____

2. What are some of the most important communication strategies to develop to help you succeed in your interview?

_____

_____

_____

Learn More about Being a Member of a Small Group

In the contemporary workplace, many of us are members of work groups or teams. Professional success depends on being able to effectively communicate with other members of the team. Small group communication theorists have identified a number of concepts and strategies that can guide how we interact in small groups and how we can successfully participate in teams. To gain some perspective about small group communication, begin with the **Allyn and Bacon Communication Studies Web site.** In particular, we will visit the page that describes small group communication at **http://www.abacon.com/commstudies/groups/group.html/**.

After exploring the contents of the site, relate what you learn there to your experiences as a member of various types of small groups by answering the following questions:

1. What types of small groups do you belong to as part of your work or social interactions?

_____

_____

_____

2. Why do you participate in small group communication?

_____

_____

_____

3. What particular roles do you commonly play in small group communications?

_____

_____

_____

4. What are your strongest skills in terms of leadership of small groups?

_____

_____

_____

Strategy I: Finding a Speech Topic

One of the most difficult steps is finding an appropriate topic for your speech. There are numerous Web based strategies that you can use.

But, first you have to clarify the speaking goal for your presentation. Is your intention to provide information or to persuade your audience? If your goal is persuasive, will you be discussing a timely topic in the news? Or, maybe you will advocate in favor of a legislative solution being debated in the Congress or your community. Another option is to persuade your audience to take a stand on an issue of justice that is being considered by our legal system. Your instructor will provide further thoughts to help you shape a goal for your speech. Consider some of the following as research strategies for finding a topic.

Use a General Topical Browser, Especially for an Informative Speech

Earlier, you read about how to use AltaVista and Yahoo! to find information on the Web. Now, check out another browsing tool called the Librarians' Index to the Internet. This would be a particularly good starting point for finding informative speech topics.

1. Start your browser and go to **http://lii.org/**.
2. Note how the subject page is organized by subject headings such as Arts, Science, or Health and Medicine.
3. Now select one of the topic areas that appeals to your interests and that you think might be a meaningful, informative topic for your audience.

Find a timely topic that is being discussed in newspapers and current magazines.

The digital newsstand offers many choices, and most newspapers and magazines online allow you to search back issues. Check the section titled

Research Navigator Guide: Speech Communication

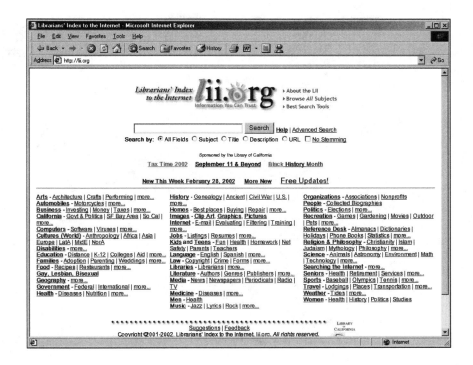

"Speech Communication Related Web Sites" later on in this guide to find the URLs for newspapers or magazines that you could use to prepare a speech. Or, go online to the Allyn and Bacon Public Speaking Web site list of periodicals at **http://www.abacon.com/pubspeak/research/news. html/**.

One of the most useful of these papers is *The Christian Science Monitor* (**http://www.csmonitor.com/**) because of its search capacities and extensive digital files, with reports as far back as 1980. *The New York Times* (**http://www.nytimes.com**) also is especially useful for allowing you to search back issues. Many of the others on the list provide the most recent news. And for topics that are timely, it is useful to use one of them.

There are also a number of magazines on the Internet. As you do research, it is meaningful to recognize that most magazines develop an ideological perspective on current affairs. Read a sample of different views from those on the periodical list.

In addition to browsing individual newspapers, you can also do a global search. One of the most comprehensive guides is the Drudge Report. You can find it at **http://www.drudgereport.com/**. Note how the Drudge Report is organized in three columns. To the left are search engines for finding headline stories from United Press and the Associated Press. You can also click on any of the newspapers or magazines to go to its current issue. The middle column creates links to opinion pieces by

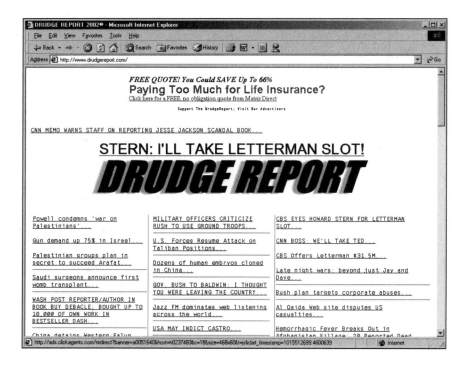

columnists, and the right column is a précis or headline of top stories of the day.

We've explored a variety of ways find an informative speech topic by using search engines, topical lists and news reports. Another method is to use the journalistic method.

Exercise: 5W's and How for Informative Speeches

Journalists commonly address the questions Who did What? When? Where? Why? and How? The same questions can be starting points for selecting and organizing a topic for an informative speech. The purpose of this exercise is to use the journalistic method to find a speech topic and to organize a research strategy for finding additional sources on the Internet. First, point your browser to one of the following URLs:

Who: Use *Biography,* an online magazine at **http://www. biography.com**.

What: *Encyberpedia* is an online encyclopedia at **http://www. encyberpedia.com/cyberlinks/links/index.html/**. Scroll down to its subject list or use its search functions to find a range of topics. Or go to Drucker's *My Virtual Encyclopedia* at **http:// www.refdesk.com/myency.html/**.

When: Search through the American Memory Collection at the Library of Congress at **http://lcweb2.loc.gov/ammem/**.

Where: Take a virtual to tour somewhere with *National Geographic Online* at **http://www.nationalgeographic.com/**. Or, explore an international topic using one of the expert guides about a culture from About.com. **http://home.about.com/culture/index.htm/**.

Why: Try the "Why Files," a site funded by the National Science Foundation at **http://whyfiles.org/**.

How: Learn2.com—the ability utility with explanations on many "how to" topics at **http://www.learn2.com/**.

As you surf for informative topics, make a list of keywords that you can use for using one of the Internet Search Engines. To access search engines, go to **http://www.abacon.com/pubspeak/research/search.html/**.

_____

_____

_____

Your informative speech ought to have a specific goal. For instance, to **describe** activities at *Mardi Gras,* or to **explain how** contemporary superstitions have historic roots. Phrase three different specific goal statements for an informative speech based on the work you've just done on the Web.

_____

_____

_____

Which specific goal statement is likely to be the best informative topic in light of your interests, the interests and knowledge level of your audience and the research that you have done?

_____

_____

_____

Next rephrase your goal statement as a thesis or topic sentence. The topic sentence is a short declarative sentence that states the central idea of your speech. For instance, if your specific goal was to explain how streaming works in RealAudio transmission of sound files, you might state a topic sentence as "RealAudio transmits sound files as packets of information on the Internet."

_____

_____

_____

Decide which method of organization would work best to develop your topic:

- **Parts to whole** breaks the topic into distinguishable segments.
- **Chronological** sets up a time line.
- **Spatial** organizes points by mapping them geographically.
- **Causal** explains a series of causes and effects.
- **Process** identifies a sequence of steps or stages.

Which method of organization did you choose and why did you select it?

_____

_____

_____

Organize a skeletal outline of your speech with a topic sentence and between three to five main ideas that follow the method of organization you've noted above.

Topic Sentence:

_____

Main Idea I:

_____

Main Idea II:

_____

Main Idea III:

_____

There are several other topical browsers for finding informative subjects. You can get to them at **http://www.abacon.com/pubspeak/assess/topic.html**. There you will also see a special category for subjects in science and technology as well as a whole list of other general topical browsers.

Strategy II: Finding and Evaluating Evidence

In the last section we emphasized surfing the Web to generate ideas for a topic. As effective speakers are thinking about topics for a speech, they are at the same time, locating sources of information. That's what we refer to under Strategy II as finding sources of information and making critical judgements about the value and reliability of evidence. Exercising critical judgement is necessary at any step along the way of speech preparation, and particularly crucial when the goal of your speech is to solve a prob-

Research Navigator Guide: Speech Communication

lem or to persuade members of an audience to take a stand. So, we'll shift our emphasis to sort out some of the ways you can exercise critical thinking to assess evidence.

Check Out Think Tanks for Their Expert Views for Persuasive Speeches

Think tanks undertake extensive research and formulate policy papers on a range of social, political and economic issues. Their findings may be very useful for helping you think about persuasive speeches, especially when your goal is to use a problem-solution approach. There are many different think tanks representing a range of interests and ideological perspectives

1. Start your browser and go to URL **http://www.epn.org/**.
2. Click on one of the topics in the list of latest EPN releases or use their section of issues in depth.site map.

It is meaningful to recognize that think tanks are often supported by organizations with an ideological perspective. The Electronic Policy Net, which is sponsored by the *American Prospect,* labels itself as a progressive organization. You can find more think tanks representing a wider political spectrum from the Allyn and Bacon Public Speaking Web site page. Check especially under the link for "Social Problems and Social Policy" at **http://**

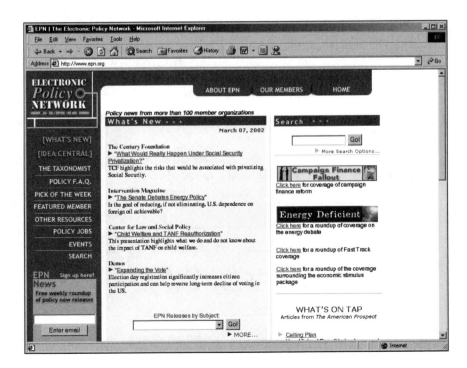

www.ablongman.com/pubspeak/assess/topic.html. You can also search for advocacy groups, including nonprofit organizations, from **http://www.ablongman.com/pubspeak/research/groups.html/**.

Testing Evidence

The sheer fact that something is on the Web does not automatically confer credibility on the information. You need to exercise your critical thinking faculties to evaluate the evidence you find. Use the following exercise to consider several standards for judging sources.

Exercise: Finding and Evaluating Sources of Information on the Web

A recent editorial in *JAMA,* the Journal of the American Medial Association, cautions *Caveant Lector et Viewor*—Let the Reader and Viewer Beware. The authors of that piece, headed by Dr. W. M. Silberg, outline several core standards that we might use to assess information found on the Web. First, find the *JAMA* guidelines at **http://www.ama-assn.org/sci-pubs/sci-news/1997/snr0416.htm#ed7016/**.

Next, find a source of evidence and assess the quality of the information found at one of the following Web sites (or at a site recommended by your instructor):

National Academy of Sciences: **http://www.nas.edu/**
The Brookings Institution: **http://www.brookings.org/**
Intellectual Capital.com: **http://www.intellectualcapital.com/**
the National Rifle Association: **http://www.nra.org/**
Capitol Hill Blue: **http://www.capitolhillblue.com/**
JAMA: **http://www.jama.com**

Assess the information source in light of the standards for assessing Web pages:

Authorship: Are authors and contributors identified with a citation for their affiliations and relevant credentials?

_____

_____

_____

Attribution: Are references listed for sources that are cited? Is all relevant copyright information included?

_____

_____

_____

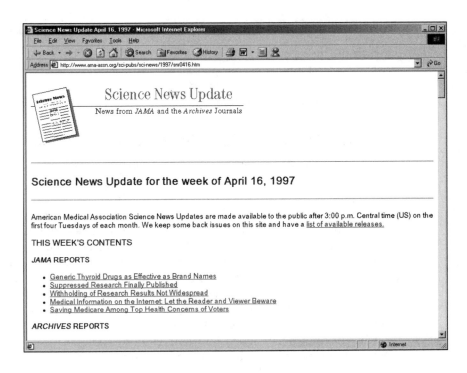

Disclosure: Is ownership of the Web site clear? Are sponsors, advertisers, underwriters or sources of commercial funding identified, especially if there might be a conflict of interest?

_____

_____

_____

Currency: Is the page dated to indicate when the content was posted or updated?

_____

_____

_____

What other considerations would you give to this Web page to test the accuracy and reliability of the page?

_____

_____

_____

Take a Stand on a Bill That Has Been Introduced in Congress

Persuasive speeches often advocate that audience members change personal behavior. At other times, your persuasive goal centers on urging a deliberative body to act on an issue. In this next section, we will look at how you can develop a persuasive speech that argues for or against a piece of legislation.

Exercise: Persuasive Speaking on Legislative Topics

The purpose of this activity is to use the World Wide Web to gather information about a topic that is under consideration by lawmakers.

A primary source for such persuasive speeches is the United States Congress. Each year hundreds of bills are introduced on the floor of the House or the Senate. We will examine how you can locate a bill that relates to one of your interests. You can read background information about the legislation, and get an update on how far it has progressed through the legislative chambers. Then take a stand. Urge your classmates to support or reject a piece of legislation by having them contact their representative or senators. Even if a bill has already been passed, present a persuasive speech that contends that it is a good bill, or that it ought to be challenged in the courts! If the bill has not been signed into law, urge your classmates to write the White House convincing the President to sign or veto the legislation.

We will use THOMAS from the Library of Congress to locate Congressional information.

1. Point your browser to **http://thomas.loc.gov/bss/d106/hot-subj.html**.
2. Note the listing of topic areas in alphabetic order. Choose one that appeals to you.
3. When you click on a topic, you will go to its page, actually a hypertext page with further links about the bill. The first thing to note is the number of the bill. A bill identified as H.R. ### has been introduced in the House of Representatives. If the bill number is prefaced with S., Thomas has found a Senate bill.
4. Click on a bill number. Click on the "All Bill Summary and Status Info" link. This will afford you a number of choices. You can get an update on where the bill is in the legislative process, when it was introduced into its chamber, which committees have or will act on the measure, *Congressional Record* citations on the matter, and even a copy of the bill itself. If you click the link for the text of the bill, you will see additionally how a bill is organized by sections. Many bills are extremely long; so you can look only at those parts that relate most to your speech. The "Digest" version of a bill is a shorter summary.
5. You can also click on the name of the congressional representative or senator who authored the bill. This will help you see other topics that that member of Congress has championed. When you see that a legislator has introduced a number of bills on related issues, you can consider contacting the Web page for that member. There you are likely

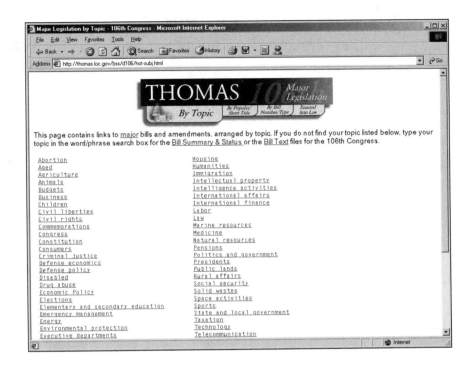

to find additional resources on a topic that interests you. To Find Web pages for members of the House of Representatives, use **http://www. house.gov/** or for the U.S. Senate **http://www.senate.gov/**.

6. Check out a page for your congressional representative or one of your senators. About half of the members of the House have pages, and like their fellow Americans, sometimes they have substantive pages with a significant amount of information about issues, and other times they give you little more than shallow political advertising. House pages are found with a link fittingly labeled "Member Pages," and from the Senate click on "Senators." Senate pages are indexed by alphabetic order or by state. For those House members with pages you will find simply an alphabetic listing.

If you don't know the name of your congressional representatives, check out the Project VoteSmart to do a state-by-state or zip code search. Vote-Smart is found at **http://www.vote-smart.org/index.phtml/**. Next, we will use what you've just learned in a concrete situation.

What interests you personally about the topic area?

_____

_____

_____

What is the bill number and the title for a piece of legislation in this area? Next, who is the sponsor for that bill?

_____

_____

_____

Now click on the bill number. Assess the stated goal of the legislation. Do you agree or disagree with that goal? _____

Click on "All Bill Summary and Status Information" to see if floor action has been taken on the measure. Then, find a speech or debate from the *Congressional Record* on this matter. (Look for the notation "CR" for the *Congressional Record*. Did any of the remarks or debates on the floor provide good reasons for supporting or advocating against the law?

_____

_____

_____

Determine the current status of the bill. Based on how far the bill has gotten, what will be your persuasive goal?

• to urge members of the House or Senate to support the bill?
• to urge the President to sign or veto the bill?
• (if floor action has not been taken) to urge members of Congress to act on the legislation, perhaps to reintroduce a re-worked version of the bill?

State your specific goal as a topic sentence.

_____

_____

_____

Make a list of pertinent email addresses and Web page URLs for congressional representatives, senators, House or Senate committees, or for the White House. You may also use **http://www.house.gov/**, **http://www. senate.gov/**, or **http://www.whitehouse.gov/** for this part of the exercise.

_____

_____

_____

Next, find a federal agency that may have bearing on this topic. Federal agencies often provide input to Congressional deliberations. They perform their main function of executing and enforcing most Congressional

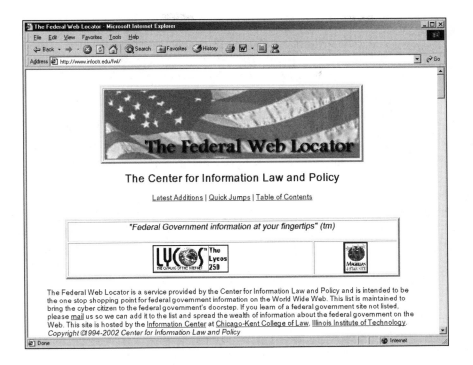

legislation. You can find federal agencies at the Federal Web Locator. Use **http://www.infoctr.edu/fwl/**

What are pertinent Web addresses for an agency or bureau that deals with this topic? What kinds of information are available that would be pertinent to your topic?

_____

_____

_____

Finally, search the U.S. Code database, which is published by the Law Revision Counsel, to find other federal laws that are pertinent to your topic. The URL for the U.S. Code is **http://uscode.house.gov/**. If you are examining a topic that has been deliberated in your state, you may also be able to find a full text of legislation by going to **http://www.prairienet. org/~scruffy/f.htm** What did you find that provides leads for further research?

_____

_____

_____

There are additional resources for doing topics on legislation at the Allyn and Bacon Public Speaking Web Site. In particular, go to **http://www. ablongman.com/pubspeak/research/gov.html**. From this page, you will also be able to link to federal agencies, the White House, and to your state and local government agencies.

Speak about a Pending or Contentious Court Case

You can also choose a persuasive speech topic that deals with a legal question. Legal questions are often very intricate and complex. One way to learn about the workings of the justice system is to see how legal lobbying groups approach an issue. Keep in mind that the main purpose of a lobby is to advocate a position. So, you can decide whether you agree with their position or not. At the same time, effective lobbying groups responsibly inform the public. To illustrate this, we will use the Web site for the American Civil Liberties Union (ACLU).

Exercise: Do You Agree with the ACLU?

The goal of this exercise is to explore some of the resources on the ACLU home page and to exercise critical judgment for developing a persuasive speech on an issue of Free Speech.

First, go to the ACLU Web site at **http://www.aclu.org/**. Note that the ACLU page uses an image map. Earlier, we discussed the image map as a navigation tool. As you run your mouse down the topics listed in the right hand column of the page, you will see your cursor become a finger pointer. Click the "Free Speech" option.

Click on the "Index of ACLU Free Speech Materials" to choose one of the ACLU Briefing Papers. After you've read the paper, consider the following questions:

What aspect of free speech do you think is most important? Why?

_____

_____

_____

Do you agree or disagree with the general principles about free speech that the ACLU advocates?

_____

_____

_____

Note some of the court cases that the ACLU cites in its briefing:

_____

_____

_____

State a persuasive goal for a speech about free speech:

_____

_____

_____

To find the best sources of information about legal questions we turn to primary documents written by officials in the judicial system. Explore at least one of the following to find three more primary sources:

- FindLaw <**http://www.findlaw.com/**> This source allows you to search for syllabi of cases before the U.S. Supreme Court (the syllabus is a brief synopsis of the case), or to find topics at any of the appellate courts.
- Federal Court Locator <**http://www.infoctr.edu/fwl/fedweb.juris. htm/**> It does the same kind of searches as FindLaw.

Strategy III: Using Reference Sources: Encyclopedias, Dictionaries, Glossaries, and Thesauri

How many reference books can you keep on your desk at one time? Most of us would run out of room if we tried to keep as many reference books at arm's length on our desk as can be accessed by letting our fingers do the reaching on a keyboard—one that is "keywording" search commands on the Web, that is. When you use the Web you've got just about any reference source you'll need. To explore that idea, turn to the next exercise, called "Look It Up."

Exercise: Look It Up

The purpose of this exercise is to explore reference sources on the Web, looking up words and expressions that you can use in crafting your speech. The goal of this exercise is to try a variety of types of dictionaries and glossaries and writing tools that are available on the Web.

First, point your browser to a compendium of reference sources at **http://www.abacon.com/pubspeak/organize/dict.html**. Notice the range of types of sources for finding general and specific vocabulary terms, literary sources, scientific and technical, legal definitions, and the special

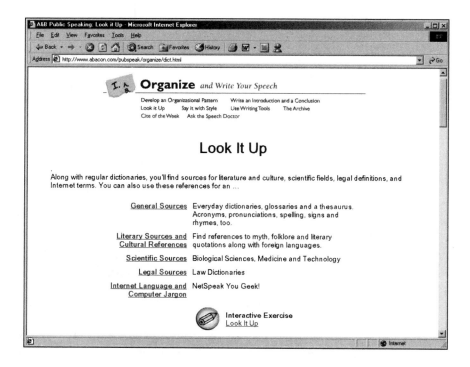

parlance of the Internet. Bookmark that page, and then look up the items in bold print that are listed below. Along with the definition that you find, write down the URL for the Web source that you used for the term.

1. Employees of the United States Government speak their own short hand language to label various federal agencies. What is meant by the term *SBA?*

   _____

   _____

   _____

   What source did you use? _____

2. Reading a book of folk tales, you came across the name Cormoran. Who is that?

   _____

   _____

   _____

   What source did you use? _____

3. Did Shakespeare have the same meaning for the word *sometimes* as we do today?

_____

_____

_____

What source did you use? _____

4. How many different meanings can you come up for the word *line* and other terms related to it, such as *linear, lining, underline,* and so on?

_____

_____

_____

What source did you use? _____

5. Who was the mythological character Pegasus?

_____

_____

_____

What source did you use? _____

6. What does a legal contract mean if people hold property under the status of *tenancy in common*?

_____

_____

_____

What source did you use? _____

7. In your multimedia class, what is the meaning of the term *interlaced GIF*? And how do you pronounce GIF? Does the first letter sound more like the first consonant in *gift* or *jump*?

_____

_____

_____

What source did you use? _____

Research Navigator Guide: Speech Communication

8. What is the meaning of the medical term *glioblastoma*?

_____

_____

_____

What source did you use? _____

9. How is the use of evidence governed in a court of law in light of the exclusionary rule?

_____

_____

_____

What source did you use? _____

10. What is a homophone for the word *sun?* And for that matter, what is a homophone?

_____

_____

_____

What source did you use? _____

11. On a bulletin board someone posted a message with the expression ROTFL and then used the expression ;-). What do these interjections mean?

_____

_____

_____

What source did you use? _____

12. What is the meaning of the Latin phrase *saepius sepius?*

_____

_____

_____

What source did you use? _____

Research Navigator Guide: Speech Communication

13. If someone is employed as a *jawbone breaker,* what kind of work does that person do?

_____

_____

_____

What source did you use? _____

14. What do computer nerds mean when they speak of a MIDI file?

_____

_____

_____

What source did you use? _____

Strategy IV: Analyzing Your Audience

In your public speaking class, you've no doubt discussed how important it is to adapt your speech to the audience. And, you've probably made some good observations of the members of your class. You can also do research on the Web to analyze your audience. In the next exercise, we will find data to help you assess your listeners. We will look at demographic, psychographic, and ideological methods of analysis.

Exercise: Draw a Demographic and Psychographic Profile

Public speakers attempt to adapt to their listeners after assessing the demographic background of the audience. Factors such as the age, sex, race and ethnicity, income level, educational level, religion and philosophical orientations, professional background, and family makeup and sexual orientation are demographic groupings that characterize an audience.

The purpose of this exercise is to work with data available from the U.S. Census Bureau at its Web site. In doing this activity, suppose that you have been asked to present a speech to a group in the community in which you reside. Suppose further that the makeup of your audience is representative of the community as a whole. For purposes of this exercise, we will define your community as everyone who lives within the zip code where you live, or where your college is located.

First, use data from the U.S. Census Bureau. A handy online reference source for demographic data is its Census Gazetteer. You can find data for your zip code or for the county in which you live. That address is **http://www.census.gov/cgi-bin/gazetteer**. An alternative address for

Research Navigator Guide: Speech Communication

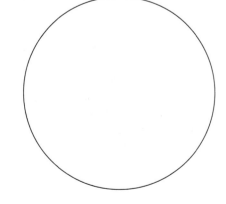

finding demographic data about your zip code is **http://www.infods. com/freedata/**

Choose some of the demographic fields. Then draw a pie chart in the circle below to represent one of the following demographics for your target audience:

- percentages by age
- percentages by sex
- percentages by race and ethnic background

To what degree do you think the percentages of that demographic on your pie chart is representative of the class group?

Next, draw another pie chart that is more representative of your class:

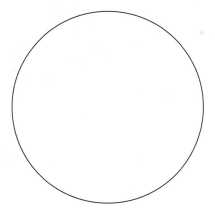

Do you think that the demographic distribution of your class affects the way you tailor your speech? How?

_____

_____

_____

What other demographic factors are important for your class audience?

_____

_____

_____

Effective speakers also adapt on the basis of psychographic factors. Psychographic dimensions of the audience include the value system, lifestyle, and ideology that each class member operates from.

For the next part of this exercise, we will examine "VALS Types." The VALS2 typology categorizes people in eight different groupings. Each type reflects a set of psychological needs, social views, and political attitudes. We will also look at how a VALS type is reflected in attitudes toward using the Internet using the iVALS survey.

First, take the VALS2 survey to determine your VALS type at **http://future.sri.com/vals/surveynew.shtml**. Return to this page to answer the following:

1. According to the survey, what is your VALS2 type?

_____

Next, look at a summary of VALS types at **http://future.sri.com/VALS/type.shtml**. Return to this page to answer the following:

2. Do you agree or disagree with this assessment?

_____Agree   _____Disagree

3. If you agree, how is the VALS type reflected in your attitudes, values, and personal choices? If you disagree, what alternative label would you give yourself, and what attitudes and values are reflected in this label?

_____

_____

_____

4. Which of the VALS2 types seems closest to your target audience?

_____

_____

_____

Analyzing Political Ideologies

A political ideology is a conceptual framework that an individual uses to analyze issues. We act on our ideology in the choices we make to identify with others politically, and the positions we articulate. Our political ideology is reflected in the attitudes that we hold about the proper role of government.

The next goal of this exercise is to identify one's own political ideology and to analyze the audience for your speech in light of its ideology. We will also look at some of the Web pages of political organizations for discussion of the underlying political ideology that these organizations represent.

First, find and take the "World's Smallest Political Quiz." Go to **http://www.self-gov.org/quiz.html/**.

Based on the political quiz, what is your political ideology? Do you agree with that characterization? If you don't agree with that designation, what label would you use to describe your political ideology?

_____

_____

_____

What political and social views that you hold are consistent with your political ideology?

_____

_____

_____

Based on your observations of your class and from hearing speeches from other class members, do you feel that most members of your class audience share your views?

_____

_____

_____

As you adapt your next speech to your audience, what aspects of a shared ideology can you emphasize? How will you adapt to segments of your class audience that hold an ideology different from yours?

_____

_____

_____

Analyze the political ideology that is reflected in one of the following Web pages.

Children's Defense Fund: **http://www.childrensdefense.org/**
Citizens for an Alternative Tax System: **http://www.cats.org/**
The Concord Coalition: **http://www.concordcoalition.org/**
Democratic National Committee: **http://www.democrats.org/**
Democratic Socialists of America: **http://www.dsausa.org/**
Green Parties of North American: **http://www.greens.org/gpusa**
Natural Law Party: **http://www.natural-law.org/**
Reform Party: **http://www.reformparty.org/**
Republican National Committee: **http://www.rnc.org/**

What is an ideologically based position held by this organization that would make an effective persuasive speech in light of your own ideology and your audience's?

_____

_____

_____

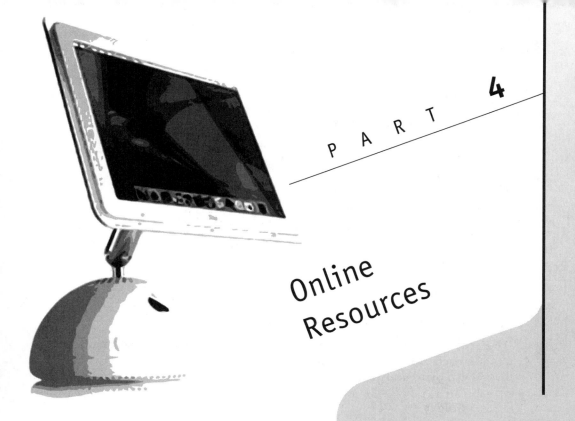

P A R T 4

Online Resources

This section focuses on how to use the Internet as a public speaker. You could also think of the Web as the largest library in the world for public speakers. To enhance your effectivness, you will need to plan your research strategy. Specifically, we will look at how you can use the resources of the Internet to accomplish four searching strategies:

1. Search the Web to find a speech topic.
2. Search the Web to gather supporting evidence.
3. Search the Web to use reference sources.
4. Search the Web to analyze your audience.

Internet Sites Useful in Speech Communication

General Search Engines

AltaVista

http://www.altavista.com/

One of the most powerful keyword search engines because it searches for Web pages.

AOL NetFind

`http://www.aol.com/netfind/`

Use keyword searching or check one of the time saver areas.

Electric Library

`http://www.elibrary.com/`

You can use this commercial metasearch tool for finding a host of sources. There is a monthly fee to use it, however. The library also offers a thirty-day free trial.

Excite

`http://www.excite.com/`

Excite will perform concept or keyword searches using a natural language approach. You can further tailor a search to find sites that have been reviewed by topical areas, called Channels.

Galaxy

`http://www.einet.net/cgi-bin/wais-text-multi?/`

Galaxy is one of the most comprehensive Internet search engines because you can tell it to search for Gopher and telnet sites as well as pages on the Web. You can also narrow the search by identifying whether you want Galaxy to find pages for any of your particular search terms or all of them.

Google

`http://www.google.com/`

This is one of the newer and more robust search engines.

Hotbot

`http://www.hotbot.com/`

This search tool is sponsored by *HotWired Magazine*. It can do rather impressive searches for multimedia files.

Infoseek

`http://www.infoseek.go.com`

Along with keyword searching functions found on most other search engines, Infoseek features Quickseek, so that you can customize searching functions on your desktop.

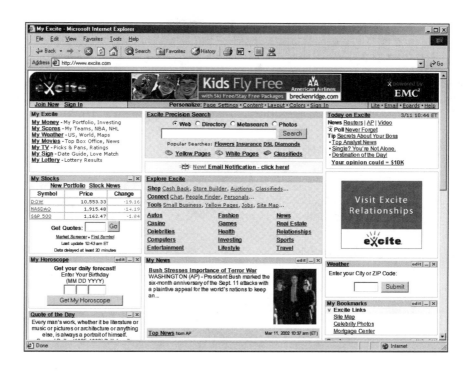

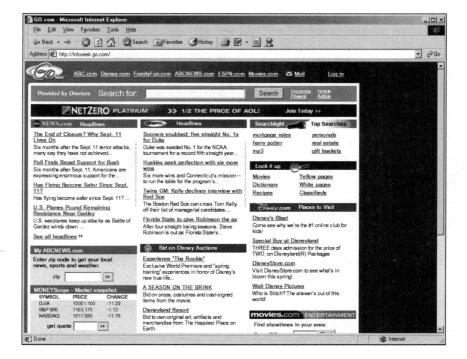

Lycos

http://www.lycos.com/

Lycos enables you to search for sound and picture files. Another fun feature is its mapping function. You can locate your street address on a city map of your community.

Snap.com

http://nbci.msnbc.com/nbci.asp

This engine allows the user to personalize their news and weather and search through pre-categorized link selections.

Webcrawler

http://www.webcrawler.com/

Developed for America Online, but you don't have to be an AOL subscriber to use it. Check out its statistics about the most commonly accessed URLs on the Net.

Topical Browsers

About.com

http://www.about.com/

Check out some of the expert guides who maintain collections of sites.

Argus Clearinghouse

http://www.clearinghouse.net/

The clearinghouse is a virtual library organized by what it calls "topical guides." These are lists developed by "Cybrarians" who have investigated particular subjects.

World Wide Web Virtual Library

http://vlib.org/Overview.html

Affiliated with CERN, this virtual library is organized by an extensive list of subject areas.

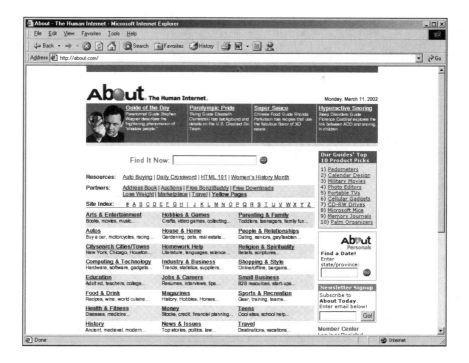

Yahoo!

http://www.yahoo.com/

One of the best for browsing topical lists of types of sites. It is the most extensively used search engine on the Web. Its main directories are Computers and Internet, Education, Entertainment, Government, Health, Recreation, Reference, Regional, Science, Social Science, and Society and Culture. Each of these branches to more topical subdirectories to browse.

Other Searching Tools

FIND INTERNET DIRECTORIES

AcqWeb's Directory of Publishers and Vendors

http://www.library.vanderbilt.edu/law/acqs/pubr.html

Contains directories of email addresses, and Web and Gopher sites, as well as listings by subject.

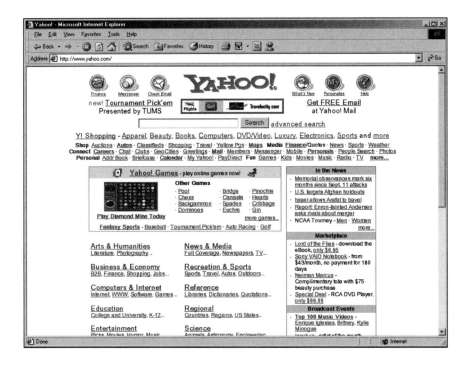

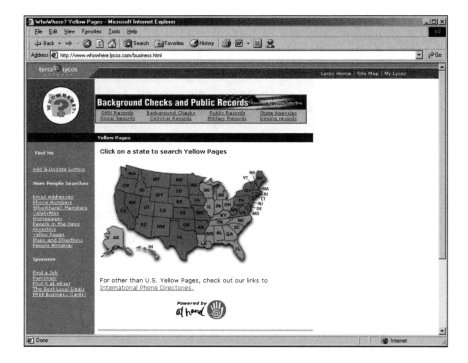

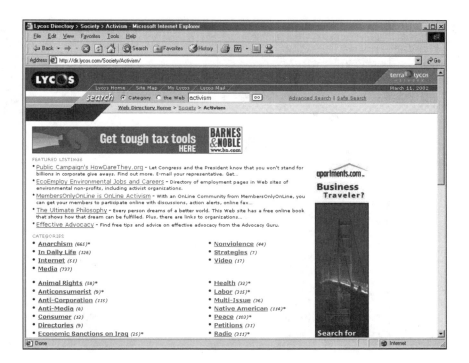

Who-Where Yellow Pages

http://www.whowhere.com/business.html

Finds email addresses, personal Web pages and regular phone numbers.

FIND ADVOCACY GROUPS

Lycos Activists

http://dir.lycos.com/Society/Activism/

Search Lycos' list of organizations, which spans a wide range of political and social concerns.

Think Tanks and Policy Institutes

http://dir.lycos.com/Society/Issues/
Policy_Institutes/

Browse an alphabetic list of policy study organizations that was developed by Lycos.

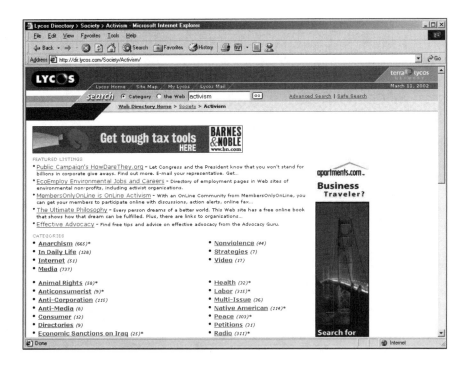

FIND BOOKS AND LIBRARIES

Bibliomania

`http://www.bibliomania.com/`

This site from the UK provides online versions of classic works of fiction and non-fiction. There is also a section for poetry and reference works. Some of the titles are in PDF format and require the Adobe Acrobat Reader.

Books Online

`http://digital.library.upenn.edu/books/`

Scroll down the alphabetic list of authors. Good for finding classics that have been digitized.

Library of Congress

`http://lcweb.loc.gov/homepage/lchp.html`

Go to the national library. You can find information about exhibits at the Library, as well as its holdings.

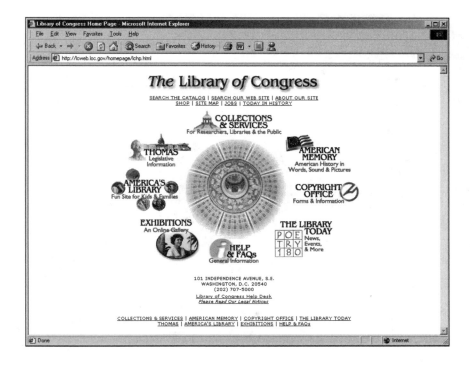

Libweb

http://sunsite.berkeley.edu/Libweb?

From Berkeley, this server provides links to hundreds of library collections around the world.

FIND REFERENCE SOURCES

The Librarians' Index to the Internet

http://lii.org/

Enter a keyword or narrow your search to one of more than thirty categories to find the reference information you need.

FIND NEWSPAPER OR MAGAZINE STORIES

The Drudge Report

http://www.drudgereport.com/

Updated daily by Matt Drudge, this list links you to headline stories and a wide variety of newspaper and wire service sources. A special feature is the set of links to syndicated columnists.

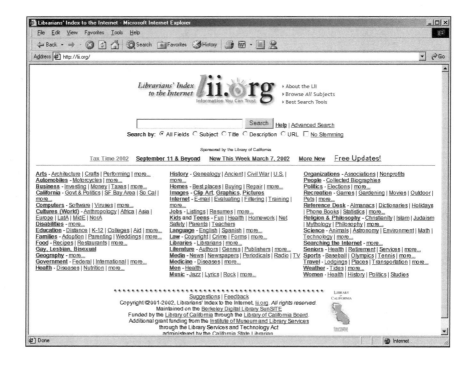

E & P Media INFO

`http://www.editorandpublisher.com/editorandpublisher/`
`business_resources/medialinks.jsp`

Using Editor and Publisher Media INFO, you can find online versions of newspapers from around the world.

News Directory.com

`http://www.newsdirectory.com/`

News Directory.com has created a collection of links to worldwide media sources, including newspapers, magazines, journals, TV stations and more.

Pathfinder

`http://www.pathfinder.com/`

The Pathfinder page will help you find online editions of the various magazines that are part of the Time-Warner Network.

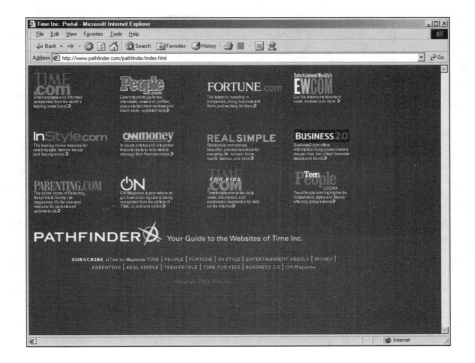

Total News

`http://www.totalnews.com/`

A one-stop site for finding various media outlets, including FOX News, MSNBC, CNN Interactive, CBS News, USA Today, ABC Radio, NPR, Reuters, the Nando Times, and TIME Daily. With its Paradigm News feature you can type in keywords for headline news to locate stories from various news sources.

FIND ELECTRONIC "E-ZINES"

Electronic Journals in the World Wide Web Virtual Library

`http://www.coalliance.org/ejournal/`

The e-journal page is organized by topic. Of special interest are student-refereed journals as well as peer-reviewed titles.

Nerdworld Media

`http://www.nerdworld.com/users/dstein/nw30.html`

This site provides an extensive list and links to online magazines.

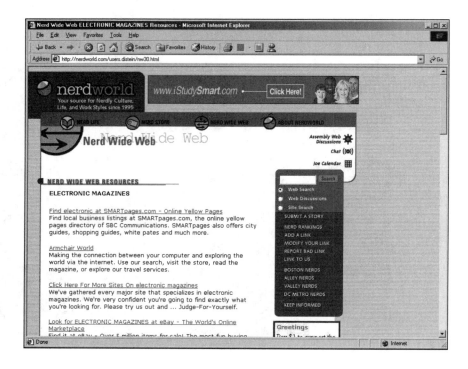

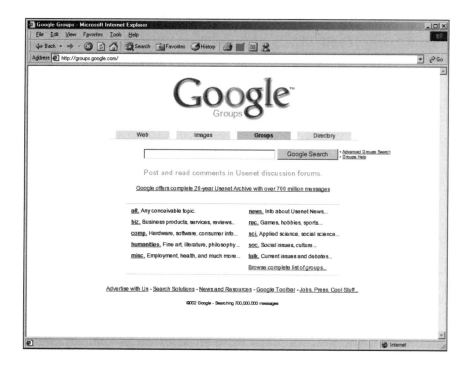

FIND USENET DISCUSSION GROUPS

Deja.com Archives on Google

http://groups.google.com/

This is one of the more user-friendly ways to take part in newsgroups.

Internet FAQ Archives

http://www.faqs.org/faqs/FAQ-list.htm

A FAQ is a list of frequently asked questions about a newsgroup and how to participate in it. It is often useful to find the FAQ before subscribing.

FIND EMAIL DISCUSSION GROUPS

Communication Institute for Online Scholarship

http://www.cios.org/

This organization sponsors "hotlines," email discussion groups that share information about communication scholarship. You can also join one of their forums. An individual or institutional membership is required for access.

FIND ONLINE BULLETIN BOARDS

Forum One

http://www.forumone.com/

Search this index of 300,000 different online groups.

FIND LIVE EVENTS AND CHAT

RealGuide

http://realguide.real.com

Daily guide to RealAudio and RealVideo programming in news, entertainment and sports. In addition, there is a calendar of events for the entire upcoming month.

FIND GOVERNMENT SOURCES

AOL Government Guide

http://www.statelocalgov.net/index.cfm

This site provides user friendly access to government resources and services.

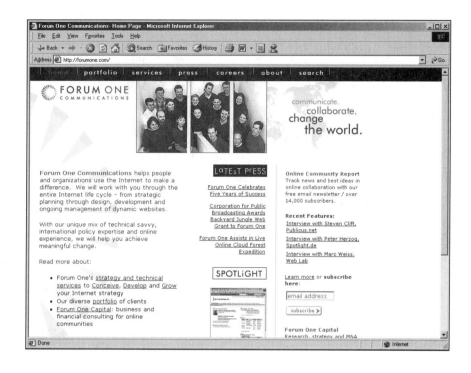

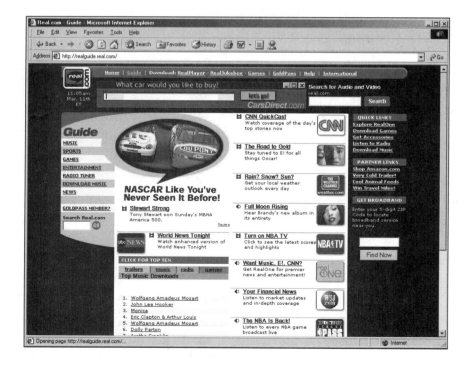

FEDSTATS

http://www.fedstats.gov/

This site is maintained by the Federal Interagency Council on Statistical Policy. You can find statistics from over 70 federal agencies.

FedWorld Information Network

http://www.fedworld.gov/

Developed by NTIS (National Technology Information System) this is an excellent source for finding a host of government sources.

National Archives and Records Administration

http://www.nara.gov/

"NARA's mission is to ensure ready access to essential evidence that documents the rights of American citizens, the actions of federal officials, and the national experience."

Government Xchange

http://www.info.gov/

This page provides access to government documents.

Govbot

http://ciir2.cs.umass.edu/govbot

This robot from the Center for Intelligent Information Retrieval will search through the databases for government agencies and military sites around the country.

National Technical Information Service

http://www.ntis.gov/

This agency from the Commerce Department can help you search for government reports.

Project VoteSmart

http://www.vote-smart.org/

Explore this page for the types of information that you can learn about your congressional representative or senators.

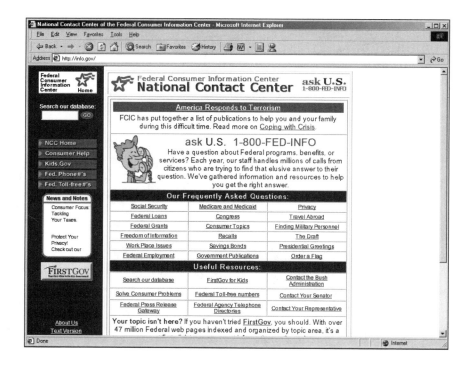

THOMAS, Legislative Information on the Internet

`http://thomas.loc.gov/`

Library of Congress site for learning about Congress and government. You can research current legislation and the *Congressional Record* since 1993. To go directly to the *Congressional Record* use **http://lcweb.loc.gov/ global/legislative/congrec.html**.

U.S. Government Printing Office

`http://www.gpo.gov/`

The GPO is an arm of the Congress, and it is the largest publisher in the world. This site allows you to access its catalog. It does not link you to the sources themselves, however.

U.S. National Library of Medicine

`http://www.nlm.nih.gov/`

Use this for free medline searches and for finding reliable information on health related topics.

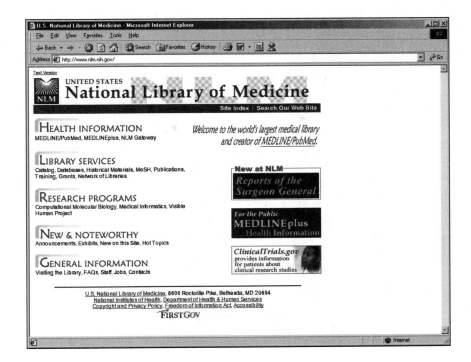

World-Wide Web Virtual Library of U.S. Government Information Sources

http://www.nttc.edu/resources/government/
govresources.asp

This site is maintained by the National Technology Transfer Center. It links you to numerous federal agencies and government commissions.

FIND STATE AND LOCAL GOVERNMENT AGENCIES

State and Local Governments on the Net

http://www.statelocalgov.net/index.cfm

Search this site to find servers for each of the fifty states. On each page, you will also find links to various branches of the state government, agencies, and county or city servers on the Internet.

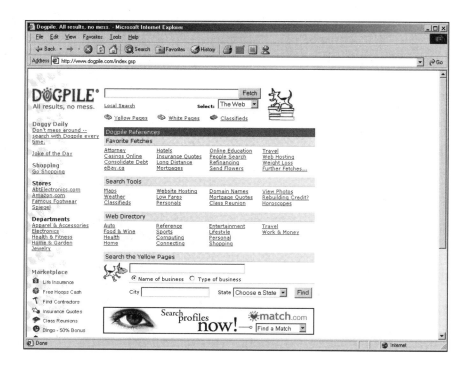

Dogpile.com

`http://www.dogpile.com/`

Dogpile.com is a useful searching tool that allows the user to search from 20 different search engines at once. The user can also get stock quotes, weather forecasts, yellow and white pages and maps at dogpile.com.

FIND LEGAL AND JUDICIAL SOURCES

FindLaw

`http://www.findlaw.com/`

Do topical search with a broad range of types of issues and court decisions.

LawRunner

`http://www.lawrunner.com/`

LawRunner works in conjunction with AltaVista to target legal resources in the AltaVista database. You can also use it to narrow your search to U.S. government agencies, particular jurisdictions or to a state.

Research Navigator Guide: Speech Communication

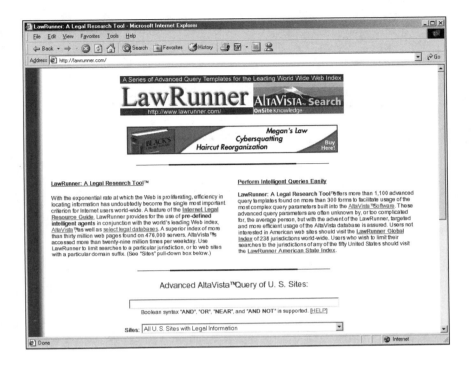

USSC+

`http://www.usscplus.com/`

U.S. Supreme Court Database. This is a very comprehensive source providing decisions for cases from 1967–1995.

U.S. Department of Justice Search

`http://www.usdoj.gov/`

Use this page to find crime statistics and legal matters.

FIND MULTIMEDIA MATERIALS AND BROWSER PLUG-INS

Lycos Pictures and Sounds

`http://multimedia.lycos.com`

Try out this function of lycos to locate images and sound files that it has indexed.

Plug-in Primer

http://www.agriculture.purdue.edu/acs/deit/tools/plug
ins.html

This is a handy reference source about plug-ins with instructions for where and how to download them.

Stroud's Consummate Internet Apps List

http://cws.internet.com/

Search through its list of 16 and 32 bit shareware options to find software for your multimedia computer.

World Wide Web Virtual Library for Audio

http://archive.museophile.sbu.ac.uk/audio

This WWW3 library provides links to live radio programming around the world. This site also has some useful links for finding sound archives, Usenet groups dealing with audio, and locating software for sound. Listen to it all: from bird songs at the Australian Botanical Gardens to tunes from the Rock 'n' Roll Hall of Fame.

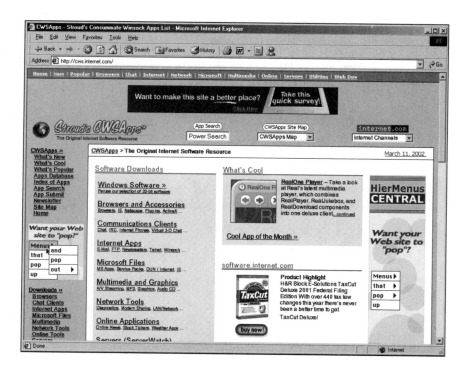

Advocacy Groups

The ACLU

http://www.aclu.org/

On most contemporary hot button legal issues, the American Civil Liberties Union has taken a stand that might start you out with choosing a legal topic. The page also provides briefs submitted by the ACLU in high profile court cases.

The Brookings Institution

http://www.brookings.org/

This is a very good source for topics if you are interested in domestic policy, especially economic issues. Be sure to click on its areas for policy briefs.

The Cato Institute

http://www.cato.org/

This is a conservative think tank that has published studies on a variety of domestic and international policy areas. The Cato Institute also offers an option to do a keyword search for topic ideas. Note the archive of Real-Audio and RealVideo presentations on policy questions.

The Electronic Policy Network

http://www.epn.org/

This page is sponsored by The American Prospect, a progressive political magazine. The links from this page lead to studies on a host of domestic policy issues.

Economic Policy Institute

http://epinet.org/

This is a non-partisan think tank that analyzes economic issues.

Policy.com—The Policy News and Information Service

http://www.speakout.com/activism/issues

This site gives the user a variety of resrach tools for hundreds of issues.

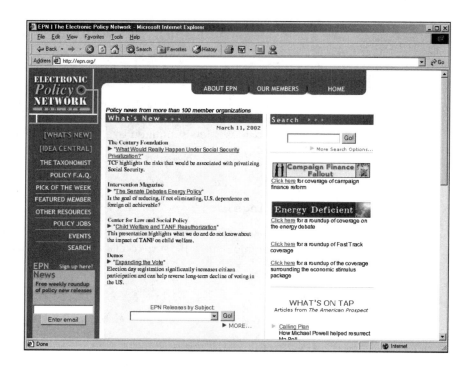

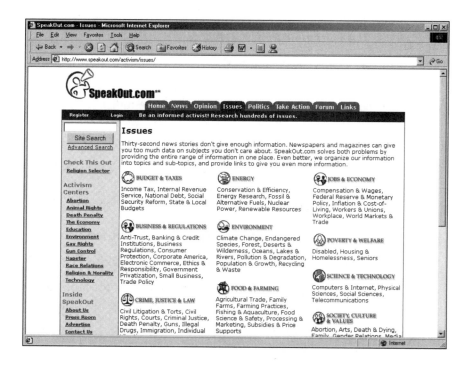

Rand Corporation

`http://www.rand.org/`

Highlight its "Research Areas," and "Publications" for policy studies, especially on issues of national defense and international affairs.

Townhall.com

`http://www.townhall.com/`

Enter the townhall where you can find a number of organizations that develop a conservative point of view.

Vote.com

`http://www.vote.com/`

Register your opinion on controversial issues. Then, after you vote check out the resources and discussions that consider the pro and con sides of the controversies.

Encyclopedias and Reference Sources

ENCYCLOPEDIAS

Encyclopedia.com from the Concise Columbia Electronic Encyclopedia

`http://www.encyclopedia.com/home.html`

This online encyclopedia allows the user to search for a term/phrase or browse by letter. It also provides links to articles from the Electric Library. You must subscribe for this additional information, however.

Encyclopedia Britannica

`http://www.britannica.com/`

This page provides information about the online version of the *Encyclopedia Britannica*. Access to its contents is now free.

Index Encyberpedia

`http://www.encyberpedia.com/ency.htm`

This completely online encyclopedia provides coverage of a broad range of subjects.

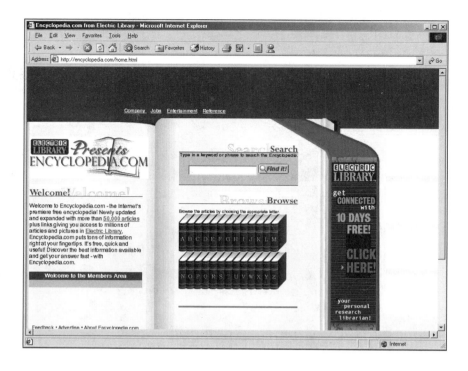

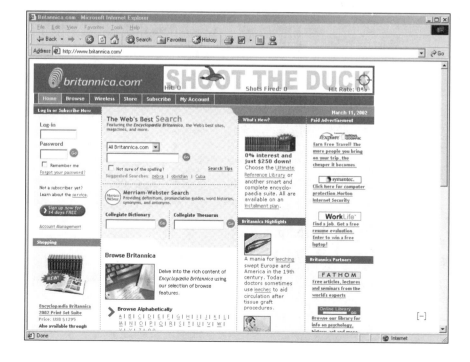

The Encyclopedia Mythica

`http://www.pantheon.org/`

This collection of links about myth, legends and folklore includes hypertext for some of its entries.

DICTIONARIES AND GLOSSARIES

The Acronym Finder

`http://www.acronymfinder.com`

Type in an acronym and this site will search its collection of 75,000 to find a match.

American Heritage Dictionary

`http://www.bartleby.com/61/`

Look up words and their pronunciations.

Animated American Sign Language Dictionary

`http://www.bconnex.net/~randys/`

See and understand sign communications.

Brewer's Dictionary of Phrase and Fable

`http://www.bartleby.com/81`

Popular in hardcover since 1879, there is now a hypertext version. Use the alphabetic method of browsing or go to the main Bibliomania page to search at http://www.bibliomania.com.

The CMU Pronouncing Dictionary

`http://www.speech.cs.cmu.edu/cgi-bin/cmudict/`

Developed at Carnegie Mellon, this is a pronouncing dictionary that uses a system of phonetic markings.

The Ruth H. Hooker Research Library and Technical Information Center

`http://infoweb.nrl.navy.mil/catalogs_and_databases/Writing.html`

A collection of sites for all writing needs. Users will find links to dictionaries, Bartlett's quotations, encyclopedias and more.

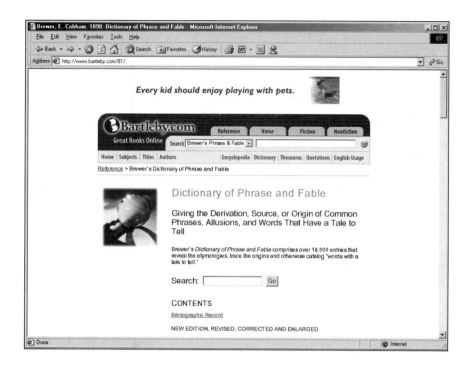

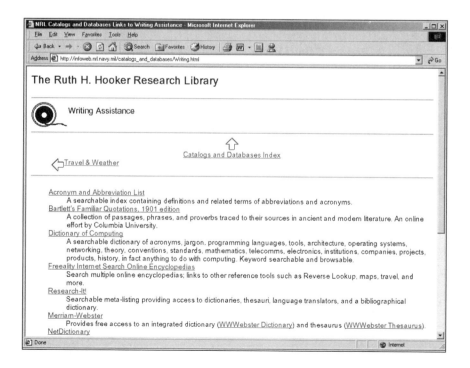

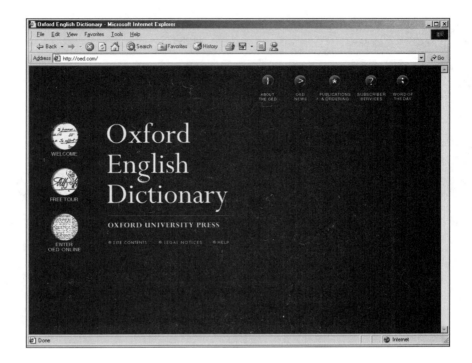

English Oxford Dictionary Online

http://www.oed.com/

This is the online version of the *Oxford English Dictionary Online*.

On-line Dictionaries

http://www.facstaff.bucknell.edu/rbeard/
diction.html

A very large resource of dictionaries, thesauri and other writing tools. This site is equipped with a search engine and the user can choose from a number of languages for the dictionary.

Latin-English Dictionary

http://humanum.arts.cuhk.edu.hk/Lexis/Latin/

Find those expressions in italic that make their way into English sentences here. Especially useful for law, medicine, or gardening. Declaro!

Life Science Dictionary

http://biotech.icmb.utexas.edu/search/dict-search.
html

Developed by BioTech, you can use this to define terms in various fields of biology, chemistry, ecology, medicine, pharmacology, and toxicology.

OneLook Dictionaries

http://www.onelook.com/

This dictionary includes categories in computers, technology, business, science, medicine, religion, sports and just about anything else.

A Dictionary of Scientific Quotations

http://naturalscience.com/dsqhome.html/

Quotes from famous scientists in the natural sciences, social sciences, environmental studies, and technology.

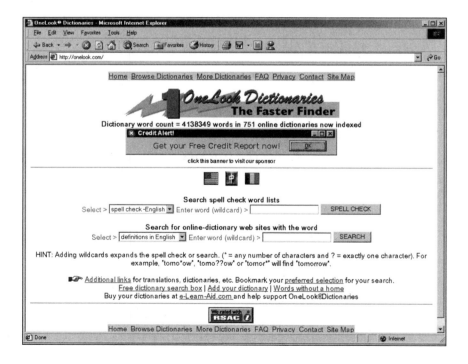

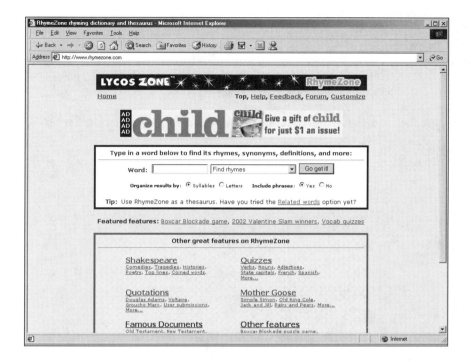

A Semantic Rhyming Dictionary

http://www.rhymezone.com

Type in a search word and you can see if there is a perfect match, a syllable rhyme or a homophone. Sounds like?

A Shakespearian Glossary

http://eserver.org/langs/shakespeare-
glossary.txt/

Stuck on a phrase attributed to the bard, find it here in this alphabetic listing of words from Shakespeare—for sooth!

The Unofficial Smiley Dictionary

http://paul.merton.ox.ac.uk/ascii/smileys.html

Check out those strange typographical symbols inserted in email messages. ;-)

WWWebster Dictionary:

`http://www.m-w.com/netdict.htm`

This is the online version of the Merriam Webster dictionary. You can search for phrases as well as words.

The WorldWideWeb Acronym and Abbreviation Server

`http://www.ucc.ie/info/net/acronyms/`

In addition to finding the meaning of an acronym, this database allows you to type in words to determine if they are included in an acronym.

What is

`http://whatis.com/`

Handy reference for speaking the language of computer geeks. You can scroll through a top frame of alphabetic terms or search using Excite.

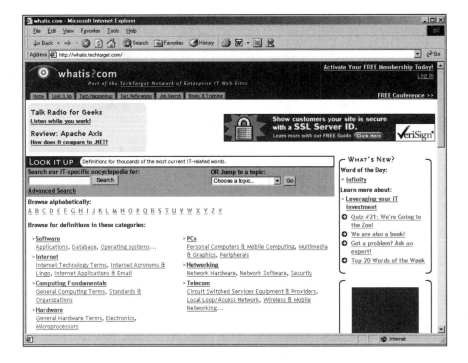

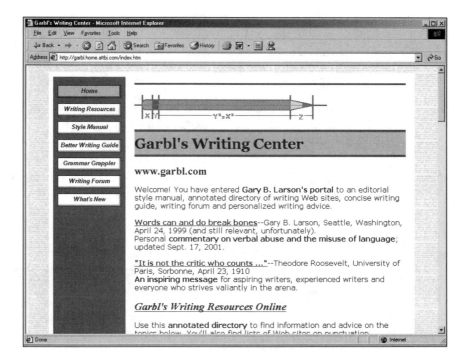

Writing Tools

Bartlett's Familiar Quotations

`http://www.bartleby.com/99`

Need a quote for your speech? Get it online from this classic source.

Garbl's Writing Resources On Line

`http://garbl.home.attbi.com/index.htm`

This site has many links to help the user write the perfect paper. These links are split into: English grammar, style, usage, plain language, 20 words, reference sources, online writing experts, word play and books on writing.

Writing References from Ohio State

`http://www.newark.ohio-state.edu/~osuwrite/ref.htm`

The Ohio State Writing Lab presents useful tools for any type of composition, in any type of discipline. These references include: *Webster's Dictionary, Oxford English Dictionary, Rôget's Thesaurus,* and 130 Grammar Handouts compiled by Purdue University.

The Purdue University Writing Lab

`http://owl.english.purdue.edu/`

Useful source for writing tools.

Rôget's Thesaurus

`http://humanities.uchicago.edu/forms_unrest/`
`ROGET.html`

This is the 1911 edition, but still useful to find the synonym you need.

Strunk & White: The Elements of Style

`http://www.bartleby.com/141/index.html`

Got a grammatical question or concern about written form? You can find the answer here.

Newspapers

The Chicago Tribune

http://www.chicago.tribune.com/

This is the interactive edition for news from Chicago.

The Christian Science e-Monitor

http://www.csmonitor.com/

From the Site Express navigation tools, you can explore the wealth of features on the e-Monitor including RealAudio reports from Monitor Radio called Audio Briefs and an excellent forum. The Monitor also enables you to search its archive for issues as far back as 1980.

The Los Angeles Times

http://www.latimes.com/

News from the West coast. A fee based archive of past stories is also available.

The New York Times

http://www.nytimes.com/

Premier national newspaper; "all the news that's fit to print" online.

Philadelphia Online

http://www.philly.com/

You can select online versions of the Philadelphia Inquirer or the Philadelphia Daily News.

Real Cities

http://www.knightridderdigital.com

Links to 31 Knight Ridder newspapers around the country. Use the image map to pick a region of the country or scroll to browse the list of newspapers.

USA Today

http://www.usatoday.com/

Daily national newspaper, and like its print counterpart, the online version is heavy on graphics and color, and light on the news.

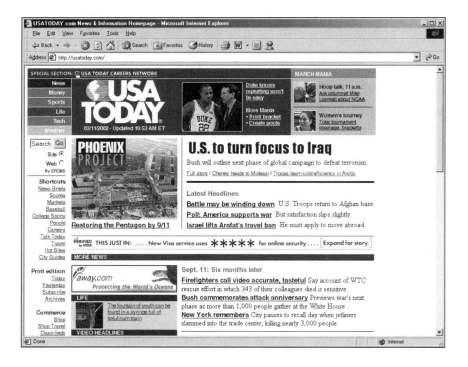

Village Voice Worldwide

http://www.villagevoice.com/

Published weekly, this online version has the same social commentary and pop culture features as the tabloid version. Want to rent an apartment in SOHO?

Wall Street Journal

http://public.wsj.com/

This online version requires a subscription. You may do a two-week free trial subscription.

The Washington Post

http://www.washingtonpost.com/

Read the online version of the premier Washington daily. The online Post allows you to jump to sections with its keyword search.

Wire Services

The Associated Press

http://www.newsday.com/news/nationworld/nation/wire

This link from newsday.com allows you to access the Associated Press.

KnightRidder—Information for Life

http://www.knightridder.com/

Knight Ridder Newservice provides the user with press releases, financial news, job opportunities, and some information about the company.

Online Magazines

Atlantic Monthly

http://www.theatlantic.com/atlantic/

The online version is called Atlantic Unbound and provides you with complete texts and an interactive forum called "Post and Riposte."

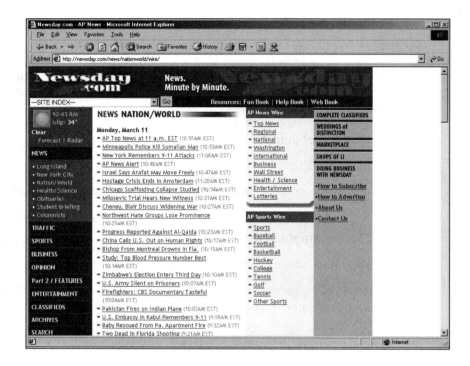

CNN/TIME Magazine's Allpolitics

http://www.cnn.com/ALLPOLITICS

Get the day's summary of news. To join the discussion, scroll down to "Bulletin Boards" at the end of the page.

The Economist

http://www.economist.com/

British magazine for discussion of a broad range of international topics.

Forbes Magazine

http://www.forbes.com/

Economic news from a business perspective from the Digital Tool "capitalist tool."

Foreign Affairs

http://www.foreignaffairs.org/

Prestigious journal for international policy.

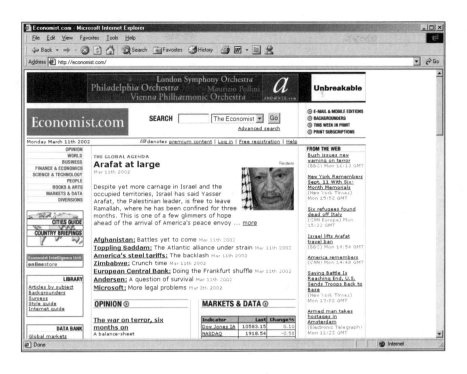

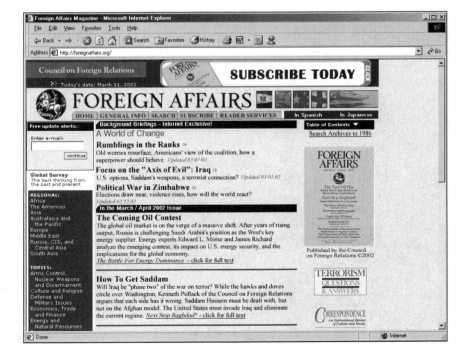

HotWired

`http://www.hotwired.lycos.com`

This online version of *Wired Magazine* proclaims its role as "defining the Web."

Intellectual Capital.com

`http://www.speakout.com/activism/opinions`

This online publication features weekly topics on a range of social issues that would be very effective for persuasive speeches.

National Geographic

`http://www.nationalgeographic.com/`

Includes excellent multimedia tours featuring graphics and RealAudio sound.

The Nation

`http://www.thenation.com/`

Digital version of a traditional political magazine. A special feature is its link to RadioNation, a weekly broadcast in RealAudio format originating from the Pacifica network.

National Review

`http://www.nationalreview.com/`

Conservative journal on political issues, published by William F. Buckley.

The New Republic

`http://www.thenewrepublic.com`

Journal of opinion emphasizing current political topics, offering a range of ideological perspectives from liberal to neo-conservative. The online version provides a sample of the articles in the full hard-copy edition.

Policy Review

`http://www.heritage.org/policyreview`

News and political magazine from the conservative point of view of the Heritage Foundation.

Scientific American

`http://www.sciam.com/index.html/`

This is the home page for *Scientific American*.

Salon Magazine

`http://www.salon.com/`

Find materials on popular culture and social trends in this magazine.

Slate

`http://slate.msn.com`

Online news magazine created by Microsoft, solely as an Internet political and social policy magazine. Access to this e-zine is by subscription only. However, you can try a free trial subscription.

Time

`http://www.time.com`

Use the pathfinder to search for current and past issues of *Time Magazine*.

US News and World Report

`http://www.usnews.com/`

Weekly news journal.

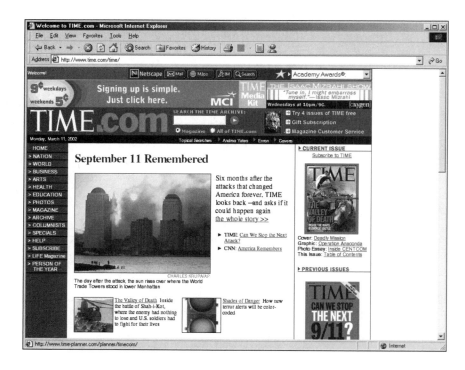

Broadcast News Networks

ABC

`http://abcnews.go.com`

The page from ABC offers links to the various national news programs on the network.

CNBC—The Leader in Business News

`http://moneycentral.msn.com/CNBC/welcome.asp`

This is the home page for CNBC, the leader in business news. This site offers a business center, media clips, and a schedule of daytime and prime-time guests. The user can also link to CNBC Europe and CNBC Asia from this site.

CNN Interactive

`http://cnn.com/`

Be sure to scroll down to browse the range of topics and discussion areas available from CNN.

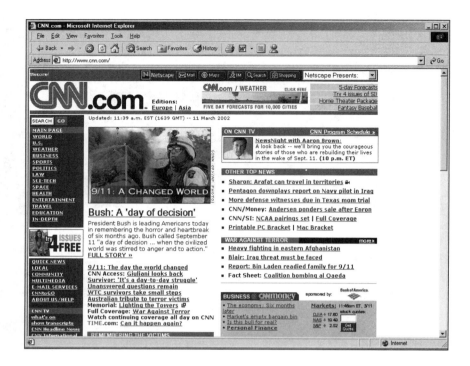

FOX NEWS

`http://foxnews.com/`

From the FOX you can read headlines and link to some of its news programs.

C-SPAN—Your Online Resource for Public Affairs

`http://www.c-span.org/`

C-SPAN's home page provides the user with audio and video footage, a schedule of today's happenings in Congress, a search engine, C-SPAN in the classroom, and allows the user to shop for videos and other products.

MSNBC

`http://www.msnbc.com`

Find stories that were broadcast on the NBC network as well as on its cable affiliate, MSNBC.

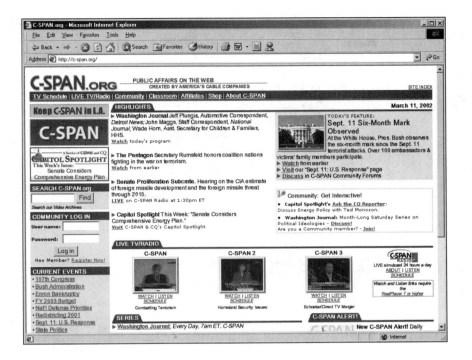

PBS

http://www.pbs.org/

The Public Broadcasting System is online. Many PBS programs provide a wealth of online information in conjunction notes about the programs themselves.

Legislative

The Federal News Service

http://www.fnsg.com/

This is a source used by journalists to find transcripts of Congressional hearings and to find statements made by national and international leaders. It is a commercial site, and thus some of its features are for subscribers only. But the free parts are worthwhile.

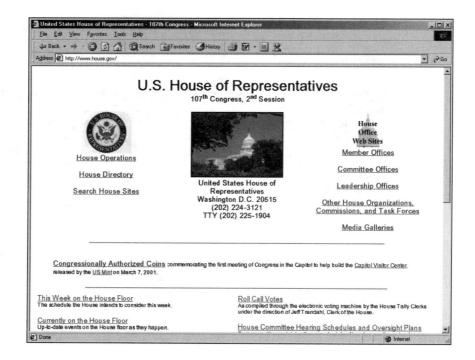

U.S. House of Representatives

http://www.house.gov/

House home page provides links to information about the legislative process, bills under deliberation and a directory for House members. The page also provides links to other government sources.

U.S. Senate

http://www.senate.gov/

Find the address for your senator. There is also a useful guide to Senate committees.

CWA Political/Legislative Web

http://www.cwa-legis-pol.org/

"The Communications Workers of America Web site provides the user with hot issues about federal agencies, specific state issues, a link to CWA political/legislative department, CWA Bill of Rights, and the option to write to your congressperson."

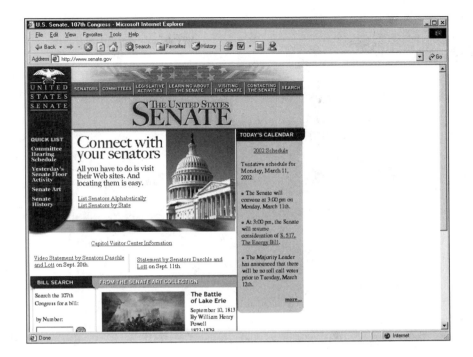

Library of Congress

http://lcweb.loc.gov/homepage/lchp.html

Library of Congress offers information in history, an exhibitions gallery, current events, legislative information, details on catalogs, collections and research references and a special bicentennial birthday page.

Statistical Abstracts from the U.S. Census Bureau

http://www.census.gov/statab/www

Information you can search from the last census.

Federal Bureau of Investigation

http://www.fbi.gov/

The FBI's home page includes: community outreach programs, FBI academy information, FAQs, contacting different offices, history of the FBI, 90th anniversary ceremony, and tour information. Also included is a kid's page.

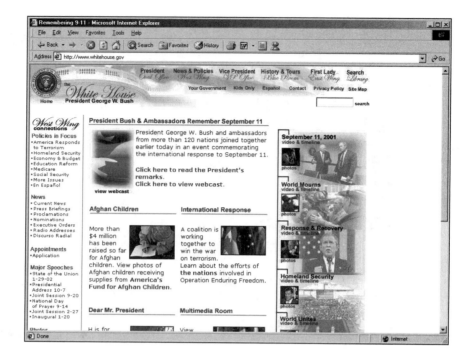

The White House

`http://www.whitehouse.gov/`

Send email to the president or vice president. You can also tap into various units of the Executive branch. Search the archives for past presidential statements and RealAudio files of presidential speeches.

Judicial

Court TV Law Center

`http://www.courttv.com/`

Links from this page direct you to resources for some of the most popular cases that have been aired on this cable TV program from its case files. There are less notorious cases as well. Of special use for giving a persuasive speech are the sections on elder law and family law. Click on each to find a list of topics and brief background about some issues. To browse for topics, go to **http://www.courttv.com/lawlinks/** for an alphabetic listing of cases in its lawlinks.

CyberSpace Law Center

`http://cyber.lp.findlaw.com`

This is an excellent source if you are looking for a topic dealing with legal issues surrounding the Internet.

Federal Courts Finder

`http://serv5.law.emory.edu/FEDCTS/`

Use this to locate decisions from circuit courts around the country.

Federal Court Locator

`http://www.infoctr.edu/fwl/fedweb.juris.htm`

The court locator is part of the Federal Web Locator, hosted by the Information Center at Chicago-Kent College of Law and the Illinois Institute of Technology.

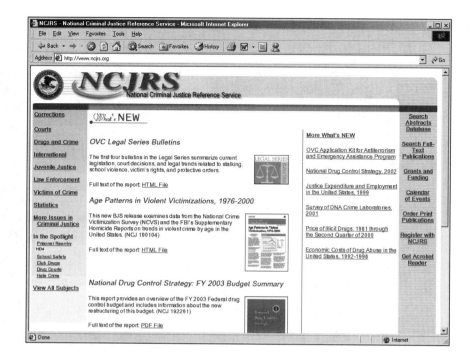

Justice Information Center

`http://www.ncjrs.org/`

From its image map you can find a host of topics in law enforcement and criminal justice. Some of the downloadable documents require that you use Adobe Acrobat.

National Institute of Justice

`http://www.ojp.usdoj.gov/nij/`

This is an agency of the Department of Justice that does research and makes recommendations on policies for dealing with crime problems.

Uniform Crime Reports

`http://fisher.lib.virginia.edu/crime`

Use the University of Virginia Social Sciences Library to look up statistics on types of crime. The UVA Library uses FBI crime statistics. You can sort by types of crime and a geographic reporting unit. Follow the directions for making your selections and the form of the output of the data.

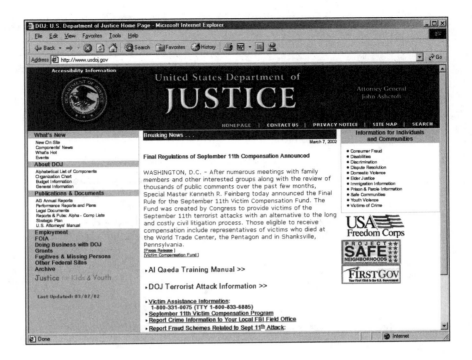

United States Department of Justice

`http://www.usdoj.gov/`

This cabinet agency of the federal government bills itself as the "largest law firm in the Nation."

WWW Virtual Law Library

`http://www.law.indiana.edu/v-lib/index.html`

Go to the Indiana University location for this data base to use for legal research.

LEGAL DICTIONARIES

Court TV Glossary of Legal Terms

`http://www.courttv.com/legalterms/glossary.html/`

Alphabetic listings of legal terms.

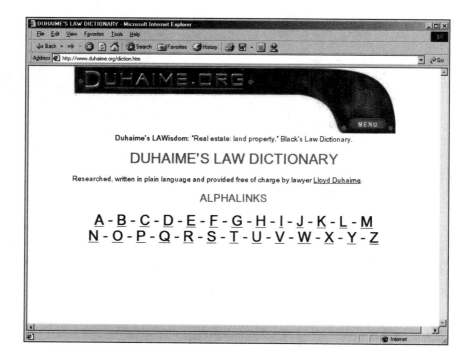

Legislative Indexing Vocabulary

`http://lcweb.loc.gov/lexico/liv/brsearch.html`

LIV terms used to label legislation at the Library of Congress. Legislative Indexing. Vocabulary terms are used in laws. When you type in a popular term, the LIV equivalent will be provided.

WWWLIA Legal Dictionary

`http://www.dvhaime.org/diction.htm`

You can find terms from American law, or for other English speaking countries with a legal system based in Anglo-Saxon common law.

Sources for Audience Analysis

DEMOGRAPHIC STUDIES

Bureau of Labor Statistics

`http://stats.bls.gov//`

Use this source to find socioeconomic data.

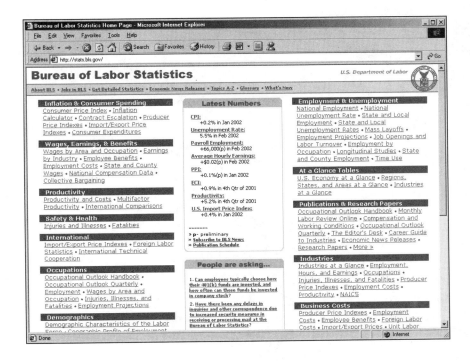

Center for Demography and Ecology

http://www.ssc.wisc.edu/cde/

The University of Wisconsin at Madison's Center for Demography and Ecology includes information on demography from training seminar schedules to online publications.

Social Science Research Computing Center

http://www.spc.uchicago.edu/DATALIB/
datalib.cgi?DLsearch/index

The SSRC at the University of Chicago has collected links dealing with demography and census data. From this page, you can browse or do a key word search.

United Nation's Information on Population and Demography

http://www.library.yale.edu/un/un3b8.htm

This site provides texts, charts, and facts from the U.N. on population and demography. It also provide links to other demography sites.

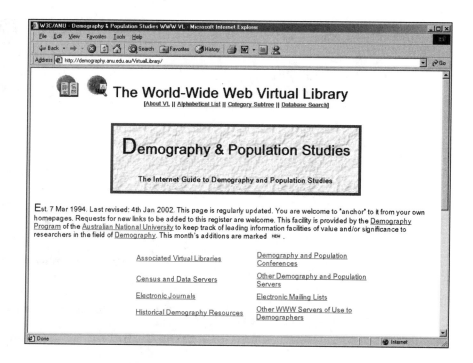

World Wide Web Virtual Library Demography and Population Studies

`http://demography.anu.edu.au/VirtualLibrary/`

This is a mammoth list of links to places around the globe on various facets of demography. It is maintained by the Australian National University.

University of Virginia Social Sciences Data Center County and City Data

`http://fisher.lib.virginia.edu/ccdb`

This is a handy interactive page for finding demographic data for many cities in the country. The County and City Books are based principally on U.S. Census data.

U.S. Census Bureau

`http://www.census.gov/`

Find reports from the last census as well as frequent updates on the U.S. population and economic indicators. The page offers a variety of tools for

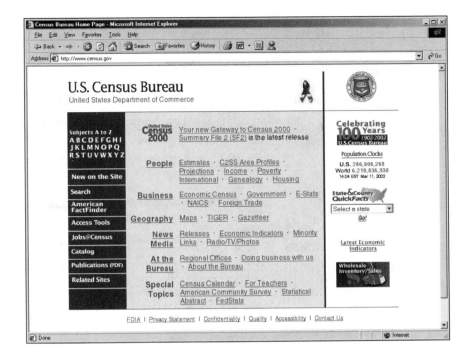

accessing demographic data. A particularly useful tool for learning census information about a particular community is found at the U.S. Gazetteer link. Go to **http://www.census.gov/cgi-bin/gazetteer/.** You can use this page to search for demographic data by zip code.

PSYCHOGRAPHICS

PopNet

http://www.popnet.org/

This is a population information resource. This site offers a comprehensive directory of population related Web sites, available by keyword search, topic, organization, or by using the interactive map.

United Nations Population Information Network (POPIN)

http://www.un.org/popin

This site offers information on the trends of world population and regional population.

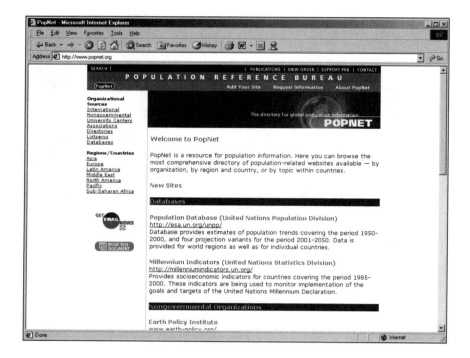

Internet Domain Survey

`http://www.isc.org/ds/`

This is a demographic page for the World Wide Web. Statistics, including number of hosts, on the Web are available as well as past survey results and related links.

PUBLIC OPINION STUDIES

The Gallup Organization

`http://www.gallup.com/`

This is the home page for Gallup. On it you will find links to a few of its most recent studies on national opinions. Harris Polls: (See Institute for Research in Social Science Public below).

The General Social Survey

`http://www.icpsr.umich.edu/gss/`

Use the omnibus personal interview of U.S. households done by the National Opinion Research Center to find attitudes on a variety of social

issues. The Subject Index provides an alphabetic listing by topics. Use the GSS Module Index to see batteries of questions on themes.

GVU Center's WWW User Surveys

`http://www.cc.gatech.edu/gvu/user_surveys/`

This site provides 10 survey reports from 10,000 Internet users. Questions in the survey came from topics such as general demographics, Internet shopping, Internet banking, technology demographics, Internet usage, and others.

The National Election Studies Guide to Public Opinion and Electoral Behavior

`http://www.umich.edu/~nes/nesguide/nesguide.htm`

The National Election Studies (NES) is affiliated with the University of Michigan Institute for Social Research. This page provides data about religious affiliation, ideological identification, and results of opinion iresearch on a wide range of social and political topics.

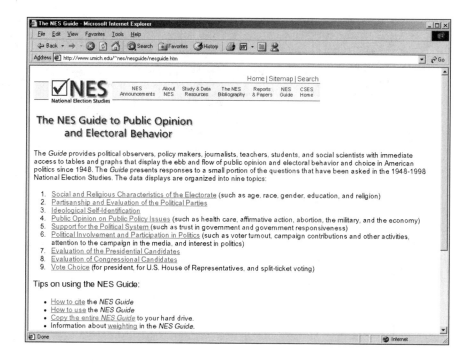

Yankelovich

http://www.yankelovich.com/

Use this site to learn about studies conducted by Yankelovich. There are descriptions of a few studies, but to access the entirety of each report, you need to purchase Yankelovich reports.

Multimedia

Adobe Systems

http://www.adobe.com/

Adobe's Photoshop is the standard in the field. Another useful product is Adobe's PDF, (Portable Document Format) for converting a variety of types of multimedia file formats for use on HTML pages.

Astound, Inc.

http://www.astound.com/

Astound is one of the most useful software packages for creating presentations for public speaking. From this page, you can download free trial

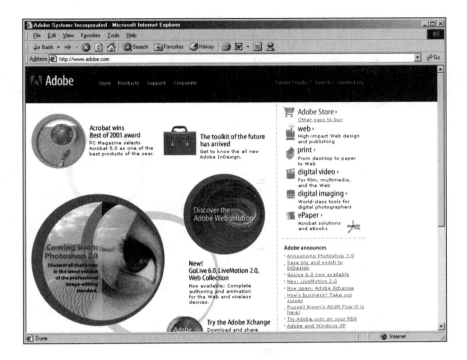

versions of Astound or StudioM. If you use Astound or Studio M, Astound, Inc. also offers a free encoder that converts your presentation to a web document and the Astound WebMotion program that works with JAVA equipped browsers.

Beginners Guide to HTML

http://www.ncsa.uiuc.edu/General/Internet/WWW/HTMLPrimer.html/

This is a primer for getting started using HTML.

The Bare Bones Guide to HTML

http://werbach.com/barebones/

This is an online guide to coding HTML specifications. It also explains Netscape extensions.

Corel Home Page

http://www.corel.com

Check out this page for information about Corel products. Of special value to public speakers is Corel Presentations for creating multimedia slide shows.

DSP

http://www.dspg.com/

Put sound files on your Web page compressed with True Speech. The DSP page offers a free download of the software you need.

HTML Goodies

http://www.htmlgoodies.com/

This compendium of resources for developing Web pages was created by Dr. Joe Burns. You can find free art work and scripts for your Web page.

Microsoft Downloads

http://www.microsoft.com/msdownload/

For users of Windows, this is a great source for downloading free software. A number of multimedia tools used for Web viewing are available, including the Microsoft Internet Explorer, the PowerPoint Animation viewer, the PowerPoint Viewer, ActiveX Controls, Microsoft's VRML Viewer, and Web authoring tools that work with the various components of the Microsoft Office. This page also links you to product information about PowerPoint, the component of the Microsoft Office most useful to public speakers for creating presentations.

JASC

http://www.jasc.com/

JASC is the producer of Paint Shop Pro, one of the most versatile graphics programs for manipulating bitmap images.

Netscape

http://home.netscape.com/

Download the latest version of Netscape, one of the premier Web page browsers. The Netcenter provides additional links to resources for using the Internet and creating Web pages.

Marke Pesce—Outside the Light-Cone

`http://hyperreal.org/~mpesce`

Pesce is a pioneer in developing virtual reality. This is his Web page with links to the various papers that he has presented.

RealNetworks—The Home of RealAudio

`http://www.real.com/`

Go here to download a copy of the RealPlayer for receiving streamed audio and video in RealAudio and RealVideo formats.

Webmonkey Tutorials

`http://www.hotwired.com/webmonkey/teachingtool/`
`index.html/`

This page features tips from the creators of *HotWired*.

Live Chat

C-SPAN Online (RealAudio)

`http://www.c-span.org/`

Listen to sessions of the House and Senate and find a directory of what is going on on the Hill.

Dick Becker's Internet LIVE—News Stations

`http://www.geocities.com/ResearchTriangle/1803/`
`news.htm`

At this site, the user can listen to radio stations (via RealAudio) from all over the world broadcasting live.

FedNet

`http://www.fednet.net/`

You can listen to RealAudio coverage of select House and Senate committee hearings as well as floor action from Congress at this site. FedNet also maintains past RealAudio files.

U.S. Department of Defense Live News Briefings

`http://www.defenselink.mil/briefings/`

This site provides live news briefings pertaining to Department of Defense. There are also text archives of past months' and years' briefings.

Sites and Sounds from ABC

http://abcnews.go.com

This page offers news reports and commentary on the day's news.

The YO! Radio Project

http://www.pacificnews.org/yo/radio/

From Youth Outlook in the San Francisco Bay area, this page provides weekly commentaries on problems faced by young people. The commentaries are presented in RealAudio.

Historical Archives

American Memory Collection

http://lcweb2.loc.gov/

Search or browse for historical documents in the Library of Congress.

Biography.com

http://www.biography.com/

Search this database of famous people to learn how every life has a story.

Douglass

http://douglass.speech.nwu.edu/

Use this archive to read texts of famous American orators. The files are organized by speaker, speech title, chronology and by subject. There are also notes on rhetorical studies for courses at Northwestern University, where the site resides.

Gateway to Presidential Libraries

http://www.nara.gov/nara/president/address.html

The National Archive maintains this page as a directory to holdings at the libraries for each of the U.S. presidents since Hoover.

NARA Archival Information Locator (NAIL)

http://www.nara.gov/nara/nail.html

NAIL is a searchable database that contains information about a wide variety of holdings at the National Archives & Records Administration.

Users can search and retrieve digital copies of selected textual documents, photographs, maps and more.

History Channel

`http://www.historychannel.com/`

Equipped with a "This Day in History" feature, this site offers the user many options. The user can search, take a history quiz, vote in a poll, and browse general history news.

Inaugural Addresses of U.S. Presidents

`http://www.bartleby.com/124/index.html`

This collection from Columbia University links you to each of the Presidential Inauguration Addresses from George Washington to George Bush. For both Clinton Inaugural Addresses, you can go to the White House, **http://www.whitehouse.gov.**

MSU Vincent Voice Library

`http://web.msu.edu/vincent/`

From this archive you can download.au and.wav files, including some recordings of U.S. Presidents and other historical figures or events.

White House Audio Archive

`http://library.whitehouse.gov/news/radio`

Go to this page to listen to Saturday Radio Addresses presented by President Bush. The page includes a search engine that you can use to find a speech by topic area or date.

Supreme Court Oral Argument: The Oral Argument Page

`http://oyez.nwu.edu/`

You can listen to actual voice recordings of oral argument in cases heard by the U.S. Supreme Court. This site requires RealAudio.

WebCorp Historical Speeches Archive

`http://www.webcorp.com/sounds/`

Sound bites from speeches since the 1930s on a variety of topics. There is also a video collection from the Nixon era and the Watergate scandal. Some sound offerings are available in RealAudio.

NEWS ARCHIVES

Back in Time

`http://allpolitics.com/1997/gen/news/back.time/`

This is a collection of selected articles from issues of *Time Magazine* dating to the 1920s.

CNN Interactive Video Vault

`http://www.cnn.com/video_vault/index.html/`

Apple QuickTime movies and video clips using the VIVO format are featured. You can find highlights from the latest stories carried on CNN as well as clips from stories from the past three years.

Vanderbilt Television News Archive

`http://tvnews.vanderbilt.edu/`

Find text transcripts of TV news programs on the major networks since 1968.

Other Online Resources

Allyn & Bacon Public Speaking Web Site

`http://www.abacon.com/pubspeak/`

This Web site contains five modules you can use along with your public speaking text to learn about the process of public speaking and help prepare for speeches.

The site focuses on the five steps of speech preparation: Assessing Your Speechmaking Situation, Analyzing Your Audience, Researching Your Topic, Organizing and Writing Your Speech, and Delivering Your Presentation.

Special Features:

- Interactive activities aid in speech preparation.
- "Notes from the Instructor" provide additional details on selected topics
- Web links throughout are updated regularly and allow you to use and explore reliable Internet sites related to public speaking

Allyn & Bacon Communication Studies Site

`http://www.abacon.com/commstudies`

Learn more about the process of communication! The topics of Small Group Communication, Interpersonal Communication and Public Speaking all are

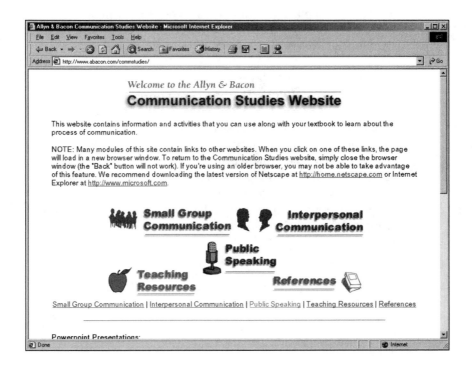

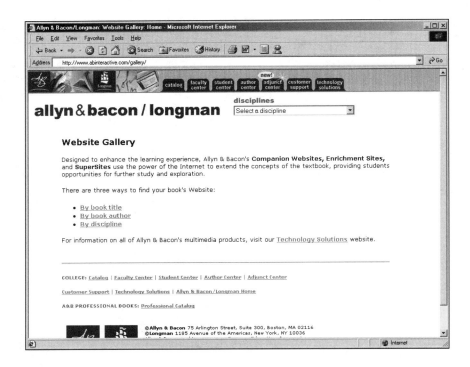

covered in depth. Each module includes notes, interactive exercises, and quizzes. A special "Teaching Resources" section includes sample syllabi, a listing of professional resources, and more.

Companion Web Sites

`http://www.abinteractive.com/gallery`

Our Companion Web Sites use the Internet to provide you with various opportunities for further study and exploration. The CW offers study content and activities related to the text, as well as an interactive, online study guide. Quizzes containing multiple choice, true/false, and essay questions can be graded instantly, and forwarded to your instructor for recording—all online. For a complete list of titles with a CW, visit **www.abinteractive. com/gallery.**

Glossary

Your Own Private Glossary

The Glossary in this book contains reference terms you'll find useful as you get started on the Internet. After a while, however, you'll find yourself running across abbreviations, acronyms, and buzzwords whose definitions will make more sense to you once you're no longer a novice (or "newbie"). That's the time to build a glossary of your own. For now, the Webopedia gives you a place to start.

alias   A simple email address that can be used in place of a more complex one.

AVI   Audio Video Interleave. A video compression standard developed for use with Microsoft Windows. Video clips on the World Wide Web are usually available in both AVI and QuickTime formats.

bandwidth   Internet parlance for capacity to carry or transfer information such as email and Web pages.

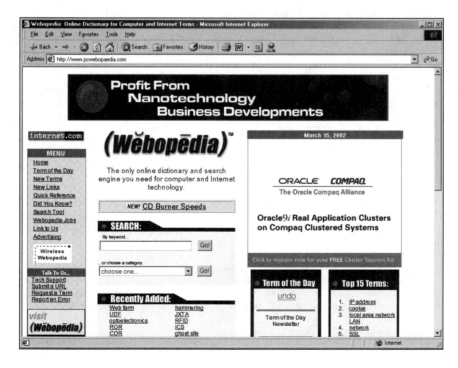

browser   The computer program that lets you view the contents of Web sites.

client   A program that runs on your personal computer and supplies you with Internet services, such as getting your mail.

cyberspace   The whole universe of information that is available from computer networks. The term was coined by science fiction writer William Gibson in his novel *Neuromancer,* published in 1984.

DNS   See *domain name server.*

domain   A group of computers administered as a single unit, typically belonging to a single organization such as a university or corporation.

domain name   A name that identifies one or more computers belonging to a single domain. For example, "apple.com".

domain name server   A computer that converts domain names into the numeric addresses used on the Internet.

download   Copying a file from another computer to your computer over the Internet.

email   Electronic mail.

emoticon   A guide to the writer's feelings, represented by typed characters, such as the Smiley :-). Helps readers understand the emotions underlying a written message.

FAQs   Frequently Asked Questions

flame   A rude or derogatory message directed as a personal attack against an individual or group.

flame war   An exchange of flames (see above).

ftp   File Transfer Protocol, a method of moving files from one computer to another over the Internet.

home page   A page on the World Wide Web that acts as a starting point for information about a person or organization.

hypertext   Text that contains embedded *links* to other pages of text. Hypertext enables the reader to navigate between pages of related information by following links in the text.

LAN   Local Area Network. A computer network that is located in a concentrated area, such as offices within a building.

link   A reference to a location on the Web that is embedded in the text of the Web page. Links are usually highlighted with a different color or underlined to make them easily visible.

listserv   Strictly speaking, a computer program that administers electronic mailing lists, but also used to denote such lists or discussion groups, as in "the writer's listserv."

lurker   A passive reader of an Internet *newsgroup* or *listserv.* A lurker reads messages, but does not participate in the discussion by posting or responding to messages.

mailing list   A subject-specific automated email system. Users subscribe and receive email from other users about the subject of the list.

modem   A device for connecting two computers over a telephone line.

newbie   A new user of the Internet.

newsgroup   A discussion forum in which all participants can read all messages and public replies between the participants.

plug-in   A third-party software program that will lend a Web browser (Netscape, Internet Explorer, etc.) additional features.

quoted   Text in an email message or newsgroup posting that has been set off by the use of vertical bars or > characters in the left-hand margin.

search engine   A computer program that will locate Web sites or files based on specified criteria.

secure   A Web page whose contents are encrypted when sending or receiving information.

server   A computer program that moves information on request, such as a Web server that sends pages to your browser.

Smiley   See *emoticon.*

snail mail   Mail sent the old fashioned way: Write a letter, put it in an envelope, stick on a stamp, and drop it in the mailbox.

spam   Spam is to the Internet as unsolicited junk mail is to the postal system.

URL   Uniform Resource Locator: The notation for specifying addresses on the World Wide Web (e.g. http://www.abacon.com or ftp://ftp.abacon.com).

Usenet   The section of the Internet devoted to *newsgroups.*

Web browser   A program used to navigate and access information on the World Wide Web. Web browsers convert html coding into a display of pictures, sound, and words.

Web page   All the text, graphics, pictures, and so forth, denoted by a single URL beginning with the identifier "http://".

Web site   A collection of World Wide Web pages, usually consisting of a home page and several other linked pages.